# 5th

# Science
## Daily Practice Workbook
### 20 weeks of fun activities

ARGOPREP

 **Physical Science** • 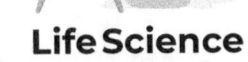 **Life Science** •  **Earth & Space Science** •  **Engineering**

ArgoPrep is one of the leading providers of supplemental educational products and services. We offer affordable and effective test prep solutions to educators, parents and students. Learning should be fun and easy! To access more resources visit us at www.argoprep.com.

Our goal is to make your life easier, so let us know how we can help you by e-mailing us at: info@argoprep.com.

- ArgoPrep is a recipient of the prestigious **Mom's Choice Award**.

- ArgoPrep also received the 2019 **Seal of Approval** from Homeschool.com for our award-winning workbooks.

- ArgoPrep was awarded the 2019 **National Parenting Products Award**, **Gold Medal Parent's Choice Award** and **the Tillywig Brain Child Award**.

## SCIENCE SERIES

Science Daily Practice Workbook by ArgoPrep is an award-winning series created by certified science teachers to help build mastery of foundational science skills. Our workbooks explore science topics in depth with ArgoPrep's 5 E'S to build science mastery: Engaging, Exploring, Explaining, Experimenting, and Elaborating. All of our curriculum is aligned with the latest Next Generation Science Standards.

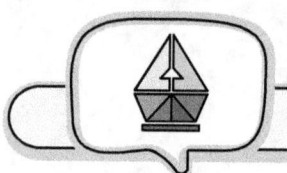

# Table of Contents

# Introduction

Welcome to our 5th grade science workbook!

This workbook has been specifically designed to help students build mastery of foundational science skills that are taught in 5th grade. Included are 20 weeks of comprehensive instruction, working through the four branches of science: Physical Science, Life Science, Earth & Space Science and Engineering.

This workbook dedicates five weeks of instruction to each of the four branches of science, focusing on different standards within each week of instruction. Within the branch of Physical Science, students will learn about properties of matter, gravity, and chemical reactions.

In Life Science, they will learn more about the different types of consumers, food webs, and recycling matter. Earth & space science explores the sun, seasons, and Earth's non-renewable and renewable resources.

Finally, in the Engineering section, students will be able to clearly identify a problem, create a solution and test their ideas. At the conclusion of the 20 weeks of instruction, students should have a solid grasp on the concepts required of the Next Generation Science Standards for 5th grade.

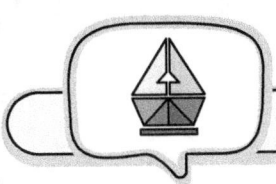
# How to Use the Book

All 20 weeks of daily activity pages in this book follow the same weekly structure. The book is divided into four sections: Physical Science, Life Science, Earth & Space Science and Engineering.

The activities in each of the sections align to the Next Generation Science Standards which will help prepare students for state standardized assessments. While the sections can be completed in any order, it is important to complete each week within the section in chronological order, as the skills often build upon one another.

Each week focuses on one specific topic within the section. More information about the weekly structure can be found in the Weekly Planner section.

# Weekly Planner

| Day | Activity | Description |
| --- | --- | --- |
| 1 | Engaging with the Topic | Read a short text on the topic and answer multiple choice questions. |
| 2 | Exploring the Topic | Interact with the topic on a deeper level by collecting, analyzing and interpreting data. |
| 3 | Explaining the Topic | Make sense of the topic by explaining and beginning to draw conclusions about the data. |
| 4 | Experimenting with the Topic | Investigate the topic through hands-on, easy to implement experiments. |
| 5 | Elaborating on the Topic | Reflect on the topic and use all information learned to draw conclusions and evaluate results. |

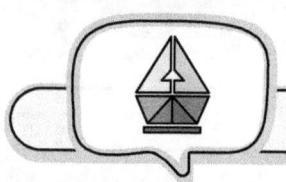
## List of Topics

| Unit | Week | Topic | Standard |
|------|------|-------|----------|
| Physical Science | 1 | Particles & Matter | 5-PS1-1 |
| Physical Science | 2 | Properties Of Matter | 5-PS1-3 |
| Physical Science | 3 | Heating & Cooling | 5-PS1-2 |
| Physical Science | 4 | Gravity | 5-PS2-1 |
| Physical Science | 5 | Chemical Reactions | 5-PS1-4 |
| Physical Science | 6 | Food & Energy | 5-PS3-1 |
| Life Science | 7 | Plants & Energy | 5-LS1-1 |
| Life Science | 8 | Types Of Consumers | 5-LS2-1 |
| Life Science | 9 | Food Webs | 5-LS2-1 |
| Life Science | 10 | Recycling Matter & Energy | 5-LS2-1 |
| Earth & Space Science | 11 | The Sun | 5-ESS1-1 |
| Earth & Space Science | 12 | The Seasons | 5-ESS1-2 |
| Earth & Space Science | 13 | Spheres On Earth | 5-ESS2-1 |
| Earth & Space Science | 14 | Water On Earth | 5-ESS2-2 |
| Earth & Space Science | 15 | Earth's Non-renewable Resources | 5-ESS3-1 |
| Earth & Space Science | 16 | Earth's Renewable Resources | 5-ESS3-1 |
| Engineering | 17 | Design Problems | 3-5-ETS1-1 |
| Engineering | 18 | Design On A Dime | 3-5-ETS1-1 |
| Engineering | 19 | Comparing Solutions | 3-5-ETS1-2 |
| Engineering | 20 | Improving Models | 3-5-ETS1-3 |

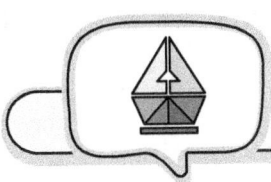

# Next Generation Science Standards Correlation Guide

| Unit | Week | Next Generation Science Standard | Description of Standard |
|---|---|---|---|
| Physical Science | 1 | 5-PS1-1 | Make observations to construct an evidence-based account about how matter is made of particles too small to see. |
| Physical Science | 2 | 5-PS1-3 | Make observations to construct an evidence-based account about the properties of different types of matter. |
| Physical Science | 3 | 5-PS1-2 | Make observations to construct an evidence-based account about how heating and cooling matter does not affect the weight of it. |
| Physical Science | 4 | 5-PS2-1 | Use observations to explain how gravity pulls objects down towards Earth. |
| Physical Science | 5 | 5-PS1-4 | Make observations to construct an evidence-based account about how chemical reactions create new substances. |
| Physical Science | 6 | 5-PS3-1 | Make observations to construct an evidence-based account about how energy from food is used by living organisms. |
| Life Science | 7 | 5-LS1-1 | Make observations to construct an evidence-based account about how plants need air and water to grow. |
| Life Science | 8 | 5-LS2-1 | Read texts and make observations about the different types of consumers in various ecosystems. |
| Life Science | 9 | 5-LS2-1 | Make observations and gather information about how food chains and food webs are involved in the cycling of matter and energy. |
| Life Science | 10 | 5-LS2-1 | Make observations and gather information about the importance of decomposers and their role in recycling matter back into ecosystems. |

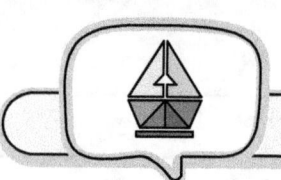
| Unit | Week | Next Generation Science Standard | Description of Standard |
|---|---|---|---|
| Earth & Space Science Earth & Space Science | 11 | 5-ESS1-1 | Make observations to construct an evidence-based account about the relative distance between the Sun and Earth. |
| Earth & Space Science | 12 | 5-ESS1-2 | Make observations and analyze data in order to determine cycles between the biosphere, geosphere and hydrosphere. |
| Earth & Space Science | 13 | 5-ESS2-1 | Use tools and materials to design a model of how water cycles on Earth. |
| Earth & Space Science | 14 | 5-ESS2-2 | Make observations and gather information about the differences in distribution of water around Earth. |
| Earth & Space Science | 15 | 5-ESS3-1 | Read texts and use media to learn about Earth's non-renewable resources and how humans use them. |
| Earth & Space Science | 16 | 5-ESS3-1 | Read texts and use media to learn about Earth's renewable resources and how humans use them. |
| Engineering | 17 | 3-5-ETS1-1 | Develop a model or an illustration that proposes a solution to the product or problem, clearly defining how its form relates to its function. |
| Engineering | 18 | 3-5-ETS1-1 | Develop a step-by-step process to test your model/idea when resources are limited. |
| Engineering | 19 | 3-5-ETS1-2 | Analyze the data from testing and compare the effectiveness of different solutions. |
| Engineering | 20 | 3-5-ETS1-3 | Re-design original idea and expand on the idea that editing ideas is an important part of the process. |

## How to access video explanations?

Go to **argoprep.com/science5**
OR scan the QR Code:

# WEEK 1

# Physical Science
## Particles & Matter

5-PS1-1

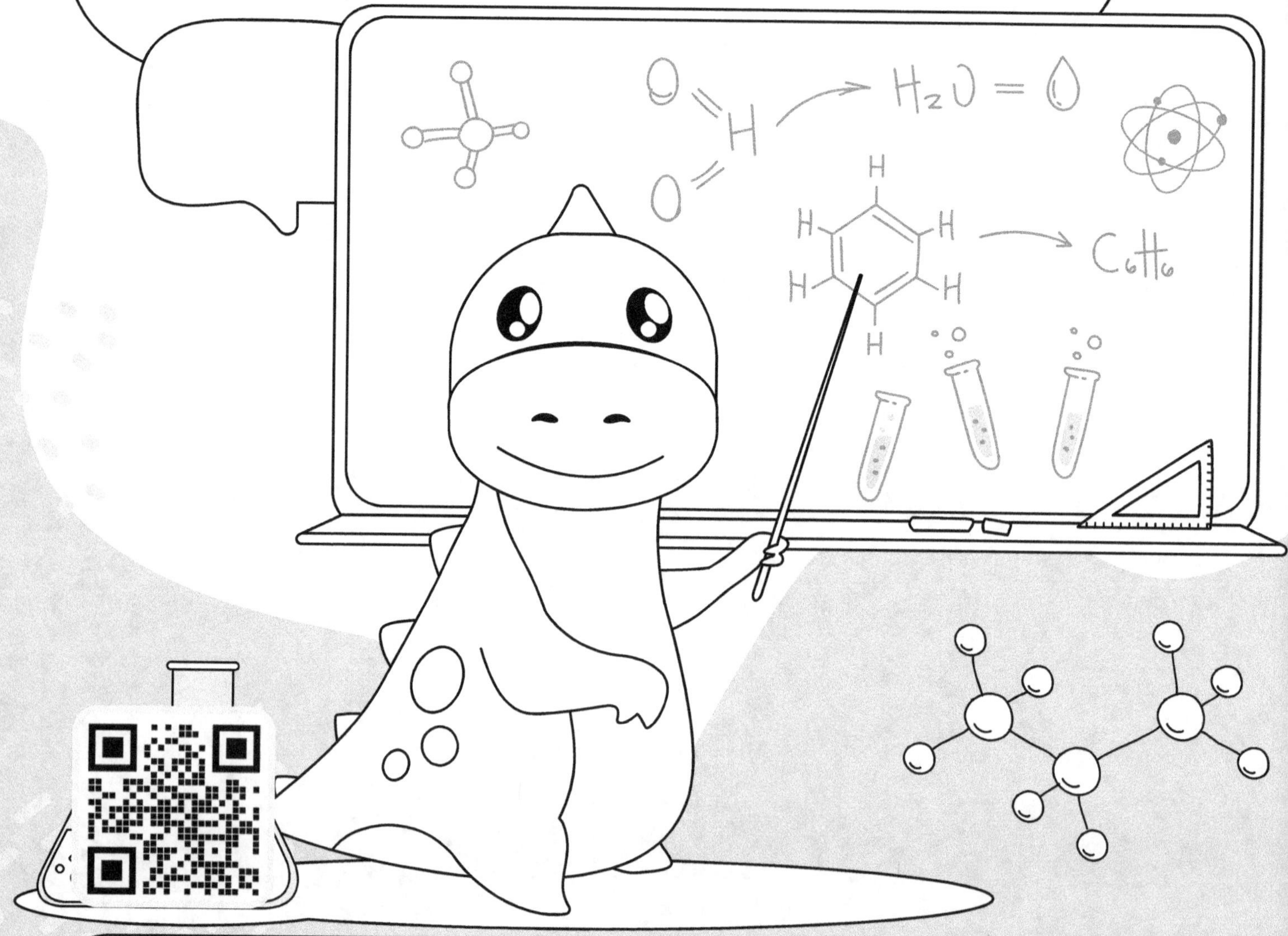

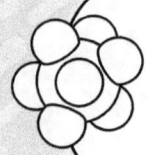

Make observations to construct an evidence-based account about how matter is made of particles too small to see.

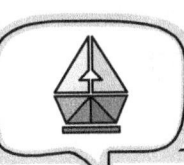
**Directions:** Read the text below. Then answer the questions that follow.

## Matter & What It's Made Of

Look around you. This workbook is made of different materials just like you are made of different materials. The room you are in has objects like furniture or toys - all of these things take up different amounts of space. The materials that make up our world are called **matter**. Matter is composed of tiny particles called **atoms**. These particles are so small that we cannot see each individual atom but we know they are there because they take up tiny amounts of space. Atoms can also be part of matter that we cannot see, like the air you breathe. Everything is made of atoms!

1. Both you and your notebook are made of ......................................................

   A. Wood

   B. Space

   C. Matter

   D. Air

2. The tiny particles that make up matter are called ...............................................

   A. Materials

   B. Space

   C. Air

   D. Atoms

3. Which of these is made up of tiny particles that we cannot see?

   A. Toys

   B. Air

   C. Ourselves

   D. All of the above

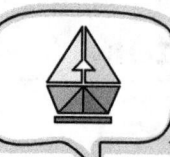
*Yesterday, you learned that everything is made up of matter and that matter is made of tiny particles called atoms. Today you will explore matter.*

**Directions:** Read each text below and complete the activity. Then answer the questions that follow.

## What's In The Balloon?

Take a balloon and blow it up. Tie off the end so it stays inflated and observe the balloon now.

**1.** What is inside the balloon when you blow it up?

**2.** How did the balloon change when you blew it up?

## Disappearing Sugar

Take a glass and fill it halfway with water. Now measure out 1 teaspoon of sugar and observe what the sugar looks like. Pour the sugar into the glass of water and stir the contents of the glass for about 1 minute. When you are done, observe the glass and then take a small sip of it.

**3.** Can you see the sugar after stirring it into the water?

    **A.** Yes                                    **B.** No

**4.** How did the water taste at the end of the experiment?

## A Beautiful Breeze

Go outside on days when there is a breeze or it is fairly windy. Close your eyes and notice how it feels when the wind blows.

**5.** Can you see the wind?

    **A.** Yes                                      **B.** No

**6.** Can you feel the wind even when your eyes are closed?

    **A.** Yes                                      **B.** No

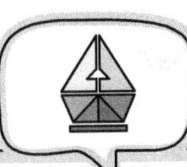
*Yesterday, you explored different kinds of matter in your world. Today you will explain what happened in each demo using your understanding of matter and the tiny particles called atoms.*

**Directions:** Read each text below. Then answer the questions that follow.

## What's In The Balloon?

You discovered that when you blow up a balloon, air is trapped inside of it and causes the balloon to get bigger as it inflates.

**1.** Does air take up space? How can you prove it based on what happened with the balloon?

## Disappearing Sugar

You discovered that sugar dissolves when stirred into water.

**2.** How do you know the sugar was still there when it dissolved into the water? Think about what you noticed when you took a sip of the water.

**3.** How do you think the sugar changed from before it was stirred into the water to after it was dissolved in the water?

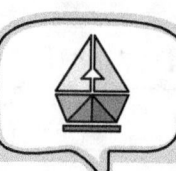
### A Beautiful Breeze

You discovered that even though you cannot see wind, you can feel it.

**4.** Explain why you can feel something you cannot see. Remember, everything is made up of matter, even air.

.................................................................................................................................

.................................................................................................................................

.................................................................................................................................

.................................................................................................................................

**5.** Can you think of anything else that you cannot see but that you can experience in a different way such as with your nose or your ears?

.................................................................................................................................

.................................................................................................................................

.................................................................................................................................

.................................................................................................................................

.................................................................................................................................

.................................................................................................................................

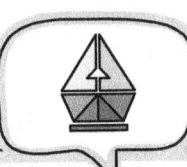
*You have spent a few days exploring matter and exploring how it is made from tiny particles called atoms that we cannot always see. Today you will experiment more with this topic.*

## Materials:

1. A frying pan
2. A stove
3. A measuring cup
4. Spoon
5. Water
6. Salt

## Procedure:

1. Measure 2 cups of water and $\frac{1}{2}$ cup of salt. Mix them together by stirring them until the salt completely disappears or dissolves into the water. It might take a few minutes.

2. Pour the whole mixture into the pan and turn the heat to high.

   *Have an adult present when using the stove!

3. Wait for the water to boil and steam to form. As soon as all the water is gone in the pan, turn off the heat and remove the pan from the stovetop.

4. Once the pan is cool, observe the pan and what is left in it. You can even run your finger along the white stuff in the pan and taste it.

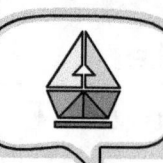
**Follow-Up Questions:**

1. Can you see the individual particles or atoms in the water?

   **A.** Yes                    **B.** No

2. What happened to the salt when you stirred it into the water?

   ..................................................................................................................

   ..................................................................................................................

3. Why did you need to heat the water in the pan?

   ..................................................................................................................

   ..................................................................................................................

4. What happened to the water by the end of the experiment?

   ..................................................................................................................

   ..................................................................................................................

5. What was left in the pan at the end of the experiment?

   ..................................................................................................................

   ..................................................................................................................

   ..................................................................................................................

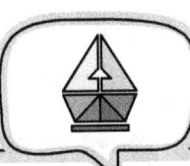
*Yesterday, you discovered that when you mix salt and water together and then boil that clear mixture, water disappears and the salt reappears. Today you will elaborate on your findings.*

**Directions:** Read and answer each question below.

1. What can dissolving do to matter that we can normally see?

........................................................................................

........................................................................................

2. Where do you think the atoms that make up water went after you boiled it away?

........................................................................................

3. Did the salt look like it did at the beginning of the experiment after you boiled the mixture?

........................................................................................

4. What did the water particles look like when they were leaving the pan? What was made?

........................................................................................

5. What else could you mix into water in order to break it down into tiny particles that you cannot see?

........................................................................................

........................................................................................

........................................................................................

# WEEK 2

# Physical Science
## Properties Of Matter

5-PS1-3

Make observations to construct an evidence-based account about the properties of different types of matter.

ARGOPREP

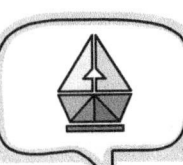
**Directions:** Read the text below. Then answer the questions that follow.

## How Can You Describe Matter?

Now that you know that everything is made of matter, let's discuss the different ways we can describe matter. Pick up a pillow and think about all the things you notice about it. Pillows are usually soft and squishy. Now place your hand on the kitchen counter - it is smooth and hard. The different ways we can describe matter are known as its **properties**. Some properties that matter can have include color, hardness, weight, texture, smell and whether it is a solid, liquid or gas. All matter has properties and properties can tell us a lot about what matter is like or what it will do.

1. What are the ways that we can describe matter called?

   A. Cold

   B. Adjectives

   C. Atoms

   D. Properties

2. True or false: all matter has properties.

   A. True

   B. False

3. Which of these is a property matter can have?

   A. Weight

   B. Texture

   C. Gas

   D. All of the above

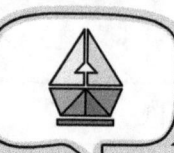
*Yesterday, you learned that matter can be described by its properties. Today you will explore a few types of matter and the properties of matter.*

**Directions:** Read each text below and complete the activity. Then answer the questions that follow.

## Aluminum Foil

Cut out a piece of aluminum foil about the size of your hand and lay it in front of you.

**1.** List all the ways you can describe the foil just by looking at it with your eyes.

........................................................................................

........................................................................................

........................................................................................

After you have answered the first question, play with the foil by touching it, wrapping it around some of your fingers, crumpling it up, etc.

**2.** What are some additional properties you can list now that you've played with the foil?

........................................................................................

........................................................................................

........................................................................................

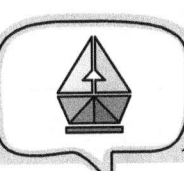
## Juice

Fill a cup half full with juice. Pour it into another cup, observing the whole time. Then, take a sip of the juice. Lastly, place the cup of juice in the freezer. Come back and observe the juice after it has been in the freezer for a few hours.

**3.** Is the juice a solid, liquid, or a gas when you pour it from one cup to another? How do you know?

.................................................................................................................................................

.................................................................................................................................................

**4.** Describe the taste of the juice.

.................................................................................................................................................

.................................................................................................................................................

**5.** What happened to the juice when it was in the freezer?

.................................................................................................................................................

.................................................................................................................................................

## Perfume

Ask a parent to spray a bit of perfume near you. Inhale through your nose to smell it.

**6.** What properties does the perfume have?

.................................................................................................................................................

.................................................................................................................................................

.................................................................................................................................................

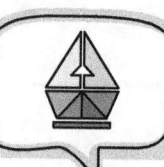
*Yesterday, you explored different kinds of matter in your world. Today you will explain what different properties are associated with different kinds of matter.*

**Directions:** Read each text below. Then answer the questions that follow.

## Aluminum Foil

You discovered aluminum has many properties, some of which you can only determine if you touch or play with the aluminum foil.

**1.** What types of properties can you only determine if you can touch something?

............................................................................................

............................................................................................

## Juice

You discovered that juice has many properties and some properties can change depending on temperature.

**2.** What properties can change if the temperature is very cold?

............................................................................................

............................................................................................

............................................................................................

**3.** Do you think the taste of the juice would be different between liquid juice and solid frozen juice?

............................................................................................

............................................................................................

## Perfume

You discovered that perfume has the property of smell but few other properties can be determined once it is sprayed.

**4.** Would it be easier to find the weight of the perfume in the bottle or the perfume that was sprayed into the air?

.................................................................................................................................

.................................................................................................................................

.................................................................................................................................

**5.** What is one property that aluminum foil has that perfume does not?

.................................................................................................................................

.................................................................................................................................

.................................................................................................................................

*You have spent a few days exploring the properties of different types of matter. Today you will continue with an experiment comparing two types of matter.*

### Materials:

1. Honey
2. Vegetable Oil
3. Water
4. Kitchen Scale
5. Measuring cups
6. Spoons for stirring
7. Three identical clear cups

### Procedure:

1. Weigh one of the clear cups and write down its weight.

2. Measure $\frac{1}{4}$ cup of honey and place it in one of the clear cups.

3. Measure $\frac{1}{4}$ cup of vegetable oil and place it in the other clear cup.

4. Weigh each cup and then subtract the weight of the cup in order to find the weight of the honey and vegetable oil. Record their weights in the table.

5. Pour half of the honey you measured and half of the vegetable oil you measured into the third clear cup and let that sit for a few minutes. Record what you see.

6. Add $\frac{1}{4}$ cup of water to each of the clear cups that either contains only honey or only oil. Mix the water into each liquid and record what you see.

Data Table:

| Property | Honey | Vegetable Oil |
|---|---|---|
| Color? | | |
| Weight? | | |
| Observations when mixed with other liquid? | | |
| Observations when mixed with water? | | |
| Other observations? Smell, texture, taste, etc. | | |

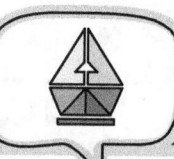
*Yesterday, you experimented with honey and vegetable oil, recording their properties as you went. Today you will elaborate on these properties that you discovered during the last lesson.*

**Directions:** Read and answer each question below.

**1.** What are two properties honey and vegetable oil have in common?

.......................................................................................................

.......................................................................................................

**2.** What are two properties honey and vegetable oil have that are different from each other?

.......................................................................................................

.......................................................................................................

**3.** Why do you think the honey sank to the bottom of the cup when mixed with oil?

.......................................................................................................

.......................................................................................................

.......................................................................................................

.......................................................................................................

**4.** When water and honey are mixed together, does the honey disappear?

.......................................................................................................

.......................................................................................................

**5.** Do you think it is easier to mix solid matter together or liquid matter together? Why?

.......................................................................................................

.......................................................................................................

.......................................................................................................

.......................................................................................................

.......................................................................................................

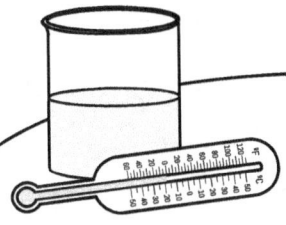

# WEEK 3

# Physical Science
## Heating & Cooling

5-PS1-2

Make observations to construct an evidence-based account about how heating and cooling matter does not affect the weight of it.

ARGOPREP

**Directions:** Read the text below. Then answer the questions that follow.

## Hot & Cold Matter

The **temperature** of the world around you changes often - from day to night, from summer to winter, and even between different objects in your home. If you walk into a sunbeam coming through your window, you can feel the heat on your skin. If you open the refrigerator, you can feel the coldness of the food inside of it. When it comes to matter, temperature can influence different properties that matter might have. Think about water for a moment - when it is really cold, it is hard and frozen into a solid. At room temperature, water is a liquid. And when you heat it up really hot, such as boiling a pot of water, it turns into a steamy gas known as water vapor. Water's **phase**, whether it is a solid, liquid, or gas, is determined by temperature.

1. What can influence the properties of matter?

   **A.** Cost

   **B.** Temperature

   **C.** Gas

   **D.** Prettiness

2. True or false: when something gets really cold it can become solid.

   **A.** True

   **B.** False

3. Whether something is a solid, liquid, or gas is known as what?

   **A.** Vapor

   **B.** Temperature

   **C.** Phase

   **D.** Boiling

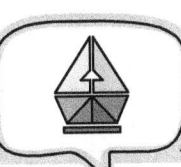
*Yesterday, you learned that temperature can influence the properties of matter, specifically whether it is a solid, liquid, or a gas. Today you will explore how temperature changes different types of matter you can find in your home.*

**Directions:** Read each text below and complete the activity. Then answer the questions that follow.

## Chill Out!

Measure 1 cup of liquid water into a clear measuring cup. Make sure the measuring cup holds at least 2 cups but only fill it to the 1 cup mark. Place the water in the freezer for 4-5 hours and then remove it. Immediately look at the ice and record how many cups of ice you have made.

**1.** What was the measurement for the ice that you made?

................................................................................................................

................................................................................................................

**2.** Was there more or less ice in the cup than liquid water that you originally measured into the cup?

................................................................................................................

................................................................................................................

## Chill Out: Part 2

Weigh the ice and record its weight. Let the ice melt completely in the same measuring cup and then weigh it again.

**3.** Does the weight of the ice change once it has melted?

................................................................................................................

## Frozen Balloons

Blow up a balloon and tie off the end. Then place it in the freezer for a couple of hours. Take the balloon and observe how it has changed.

**4.** What does the balloon look like after being in the freezer for a couple of hours?

................................................................................................................

................................................................................................................

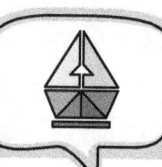
*Yesterday, you explored how temperature affects the properties of solid, liquids, and gases. Today you will elaborate on your findings and explain these phenomena.*

**Directions:** Read each text below. Then answer the questions that follow.

## Chill Out!

You discovered that ice takes up more volume than liquid water.

**1.** How does freezing water change its properties?

......................................................................................................................

......................................................................................................................

......................................................................................................................

......................................................................................................................

## Chill Out: Part 2

You discovered even though ice takes up more space, when it melts and becomes a liquid, it weighs the same.

**2.** Why do you think the ice weighs the same as the liquid water it becomes when it melts/warms up?

......................................................................................................................

......................................................................................................................

......................................................................................................................

......................................................................................................................

## Frozen Balloons

You discovered that balloons shrink when placed in the freezer.

**3.** What is happening to the air inside the balloon when it gets cold in the freezer?

......................................................................................................................

......................................................................................................................

......................................................................................................................

......................................................................................................................

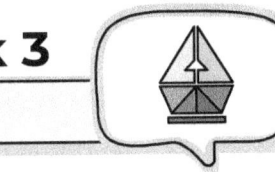
*You have spent a few days exploring how heat and cold affect the properties of matter and the phases of matter. Today you will experiment further with these concepts.*

## Materials:

1. Water
2. Juice (any flavor)
3. Salt
4. 3 identical clear cups (microwave-safe)
5. Spoons for stirring
6. Measuring cups/measuring spoons
7. Thermometer

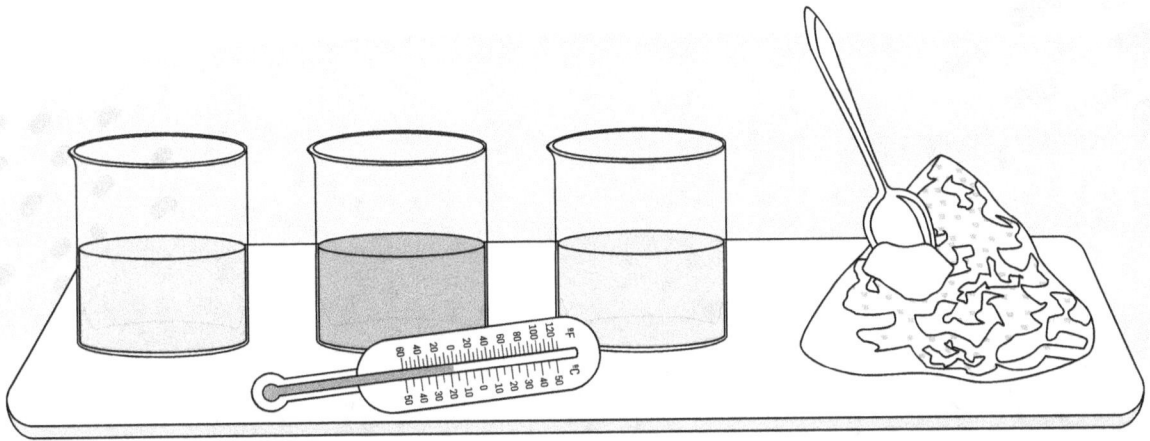

## Procedure:

1. Measure out $\frac{1}{2}$ cup of water into two of the clear cups. In one of the cups of water add 2 tablespoons of salt and stir until it's dissolved.

2. Measure out $\frac{1}{2}$ cup of juice into the third clear cup.

3. Leave the cups out on the kitchen counter until they are the same temperature when you place a thermometer into each cup.

4. Place all of the cups into the freezer for 2 hours, measuring the temperature every 30 minutes. Note if and when any of the cups start to turn icy.

5. Place all of the cups in the microwave at the same time and microwave on high for 15 seconds. Take the temperature of each cup. Place the cups back in the microwave and repeat this step, taking the temperature each time, until all of the cups contain nothing but liquid. In other words, you are trying to melt any ice that formed during step #4 of this experiment.

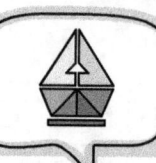
**Follow-up Questions:**

**1.** What is one property of each of the cups of liquid?

.................................................................................................

.................................................................................................

**2.** Which cup started to become icy first?

.................................................................................................

.................................................................................................

**3.** Did any of the cups freeze solid in the two hours?

.................................................................................................

.................................................................................................

**4.** Which liquid melted quickest in the microwave?

.................................................................................................

.................................................................................................

*Yesterday, you experimented with honey and vegetable oil, recording their properties as you went. Today you will elaborate on these properties that you discovered last lesson.*

**Directions:** Read and answer each question below.

1. Do you think the volume of the liquids in each cup was different at the end of the experiment compared to at the beginning of the experiment? Why or why not?

........................................................................................................

........................................................................................................

........................................................................................................

........................................................................................................

2. Why do you think the cup with only water became icy quickest when it was placed in the freezer?

........................................................................................................

........................................................................................................

........................................................................................................

........................................................................................................

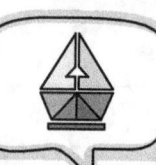
**3.** Does temperature affect different kinds of matter in the same way, even if the matter is in the same phase such as liquid?

.............................................................................................................

.............................................................................................................

.............................................................................................................

.............................................................................................................

**4.** If you started with boiling water in the cups, would placing it in the freezer still cause it to freeze into a solid at some point?

.............................................................................................................

.............................................................................................................

# Physical Science

## Gravity

5-PS2-1

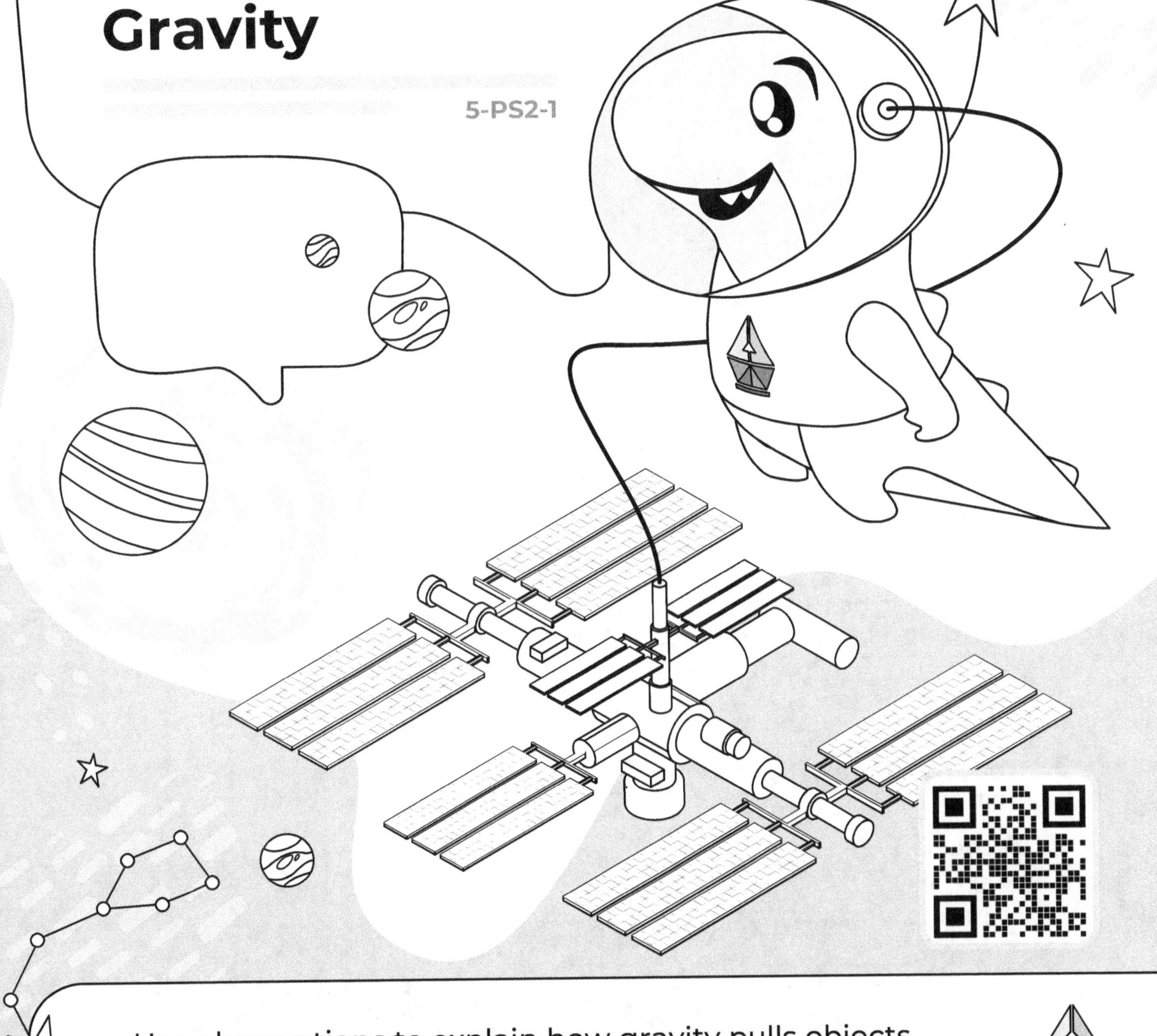

Use observations to explain how gravity pulls objects down towards Earth.

ARGOPREP

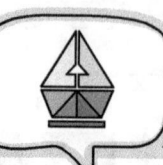
**Directions:** Read the text below. Then answer the questions that follow.

## The Power Of Gravity

Have you ever wondered why when you jump, you always land back on the ground? Why don't you fly off into space? Or perhaps you've wondered why a ball will always fall back to Earth no matter how hard or high up in the air you throw it. The answer to these questions is the same: **gravity**. Gravity is the force which draws objects down towards Earth. Earth has gravity because Earth is huge and contains a huge amount of matter. All of Earth's matter gives it **mass**. If something has a lot of mass, it tends to have a lot of gravity and can pull things towards it. How much force something has in this situation is called **gravitational force**. If something does not have much mass, it does not have as much gravity and pulls things towards it with much less force. The Sun is huge and therefore has gravity which is why all of the planets in our solar system orbit the Sun. Earth is much smaller than Earth and therefore has less gravity - this is why our small moon orbits us but not other planets.

**1.** When an acorn falls from an Oak tree onto the ground, this is caused by what force?

    **A.** Mass                 **C.** The Sun

    **B.** Gravity             **D.** Matter

**2.** If something has more _____, it has more gravity and pulls things towards itself with more force.

    **A.** Matter             **C.** Moons

    **B.** Mass               **D.** Gravity

**3.** What has the most gravity in our solar system and therefore has many planets orbiting it?

    **A.** The Sun           **C.** Our moon

    **B.** Earth              **D.** Space

*Yesterday, you learned what gravity is and how things with more mass tend to have more gravitational force on objects around them. Today you will explore this phenomenon in your own home.*

**Directions:** Read each text below and complete the activity. Then answer the questions that follow.

## Bouncing Balls

Go into your driveway with a tennis ball and release it from your hand right in front of you. Do this a few more times and notice where the ball ends up each time.

**1.** Where does the ball always end up every time you let go of it?

## Heavy Vs. Light Objects

Take a paperclip and a full, unopened water bottle in each of your hands. Go outside so that you are standing on grass and hold them out straight in front of you with your arms fully extended. Count to three and then drop them at the same time. Notice when each one hits the ground. Repeat a few times to see if you get the same results.

**2.** Which of the two objects is heavier?

**3.** Did the two objects hit the ground at the same time or at different times?

## Up In The Air

Take the same paperclip and plastic bottle from the last demo outside onto a spot with grass. Hold each object one at a time down by your side. Use some effort and toss each one into the air, releasing the object when your arm extends to about shoulder height. Do this a few times with each object and notice how high each object goes when you toss it upwards with roughly the same amount of effort.

**4.** Which object travels higher in the sky when you throw it with the same amount of force?

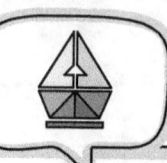
*Yesterday, you explored how gravity affects different everyday objects. Today you will explain some of the observations you made about mass and gravitational force.*

**Directions:** Read each text below. Then answer the questions that follow.

## Bouncing Balls

You discovered when a tennis ball is dropped, it will always end up on the ground.

**1.** What force is causing the ball to always end up on the ground?

## Heavy Vs. Light Objects

You discovered when two objects are dropped from the same height, they will land on the ground at about the same time regardless of their weight.

**2.** Do you think gravity affects light and heavy objects the same or differently?

## Up In The Air

You discovered that heavy objects and light objects will land on the ground at the same time if they are dropped at the same time.

**3.** If you wanted a heavy object to travel as high as a light object when you toss it, what must you do?

*You have explored how gravity affects objects of different mass over the past couple of lessons. Today you will experiment more with these concepts.*

### Materials:

1. A computer with the Internet
2. A notepad
3. A pencil

### Procedure:

1. Find a couple of videos on the Internet of astronauts in space. The NASA website is a great resource as is YouTube.

   A. Find one video of astronauts walking on the moon. It is best to find a video where there are also examples of them jumping.

   B. Fine one video of astronauts doing something inside of a space station or a spaceship.

2. As you watch, observe and write down anything you notice about how the astronauts move or how objects move in space.

3. After, watch a few videos of people walking around or jumping here on Earth. As you watch, write down notes about how they move or how objects around them move on Earth.

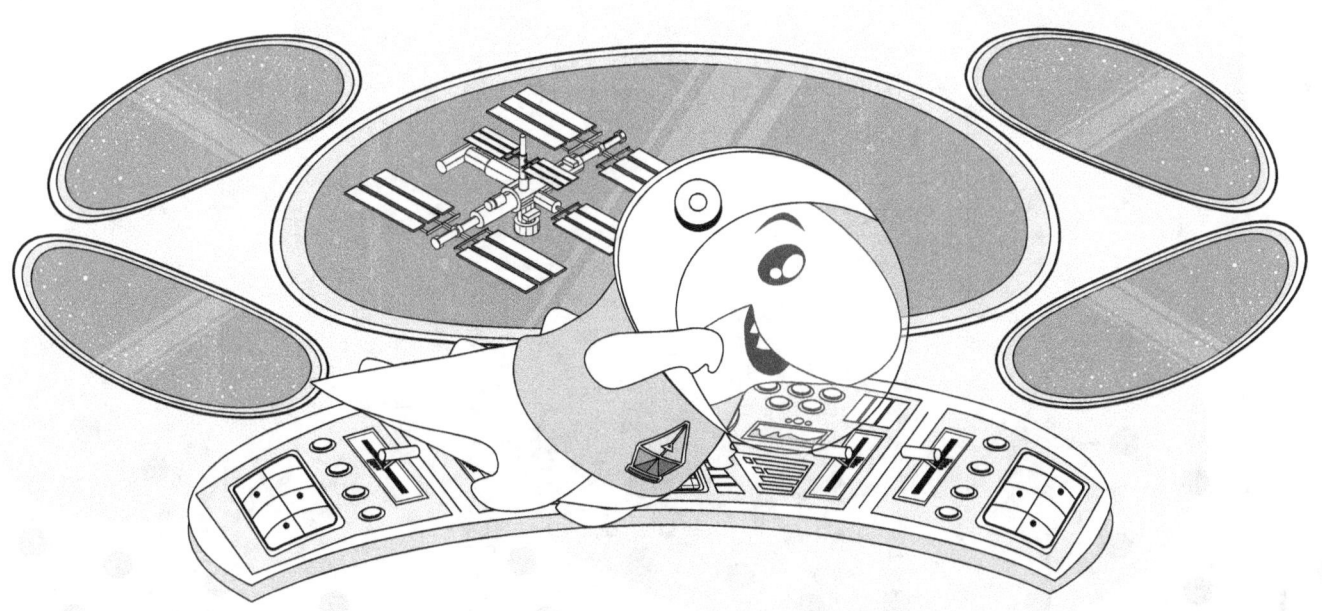

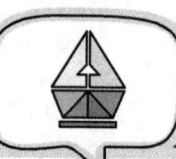
### Follow-up Questions:

**1.** When an astronaut jumps and walks on the moon, what do you notice?

.................................................................................................................................

.................................................................................................................................

.................................................................................................................................

**2.** When an astronaut does something inside of a space station, what do you notice?

.................................................................................................................................

.................................................................................................................................

.................................................................................................................................

**3.** How does walking and jumping on Earth compare to walking and jumping in space based on the observations you made?

.................................................................................................................................

.................................................................................................................................

.................................................................................................................................

**4.** Do you think it is easier to jump on the moon or on Earth based on your observations?

.................................................................................................................................

.................................................................................................................................

.................................................................................................................................

*Yesterday, you observed how gravity works in space and on the moon compared to how gravity works on Earth. Today you will elaborate on those observations.*

**Directions:** Read and answer each question below.

1. Based on your observations, do you think the gravitational force of Earth is more or less than the gravitational force of the moon? Why?

2. If you dropped a bowling ball on the moon, do you think it would fall faster or slower to the moon's surface than on Earth?

3. What is one problem astronauts might have working in space because of the lack of gravity?

4. Mercury is the smallest planet in our solar system. Do you think it has more gravity or less gravity than Earth? Do you think it has more gravity or less gravity than the Sun?

# WEEK 5

# Physical Science
## Chemical Reactions

5-PS1-4

Make observations to construct an evidence-based account about how chemical reactions create new substances.

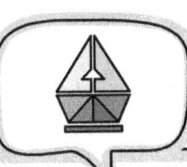
**Directions:** Read the text below. Then answer the questions that follow.

# The Magic Of Chemical Reactions

Take a moment and consider your favorite baked good - perhaps it's a type of cookie, a cake, or some other sort of baked good. Now think about how it is made. You start by mixing ingredients together such as flour, sugar, eggs and other things. You put it in the oven and once it comes out, you have a delicious treat that is very different from the dough or batter you had before. So what happened?

A **chemical reaction** is a process that takes matter and reorganizes it into a new type of matter. The matter that goes into a chemical reaction is known as the **reactants**. In the example of the baked good the reactants would be each of the ingredients like the flour, sugar and eggs. The matter that is a result of the chemical reaction is known as the **product**. In this example the cake is the product. Heat from the oven helps power the chemical reaction.

1. Baking a cake would be considered what type of process?

   **A.** Matter

   **B.** Reactants

   **C.** Products

   **D.** Chemical Reaction

2. What do you call the matter that goes into a chemical reaction?

   **A.** Matter

   **B.** Reactants

   **C.** Products

   **D.** Chemical Reaction

3. What do you call the matter that is a result of a chemical reaction?

   **A.** Matter

   **B.** Reactants

   **C.** Products

   **D.** Chemical Reaction

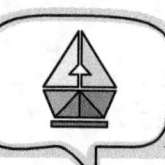
*Yesterday, you learned about the process known as a chemical reaction. Today you will explore a few chemical reactions and make observations.*

**Directions:** Read each text below and complete the activity. Then answer the question that follows.

### A Classic Experiment: Part 1

Take a large clear glass and place it on a plate. Place 1 tablespoon of baking soda in the glass. Then measure out 1 tablespoon of vinegar and pour it into the glass. Do not stir the contents of the glass, simply observe what happens.

**1.** What does the baking soda look like when you place it in the glass by itself?

**2.** Do you think you saw a chemical reaction happen?

A. Yes

B. No

### A Classic Experiment: Part 2

Clean out the glass from the previous experiment and dry it, placing it back on the plate in case anything spills. Now place 3 tablespoons of baking soda in the glass. Then measure 3 tablespoons of vinegar and put it into the glass. Do not stir it and watch what happens.

**3.** Do you think you saw a chemical reaction happen?

A. Yes

B. No

### A Classic Experiment: Part 3

Clean out the glass from the previous experiment and dry it, placing it back on the plate in case anything spills. Now place 3 tablespoons of baking soda in the glass. This time, measure only only 1 tablespoon of vinegar and put it into the glass. Do not stir it and watch what happens.

**4.** Is there any baking soda left in the glass by the end of the experiment?

A. Yes

B. No

*Yesterday, you explored the chemical reaction that occurs when vinegar and baking soda are mixed together. Today you will elaborate on these observations.*

**Directions:** Read each text below. Then answer the questions that follow.

## A Classic Experiment: Part 1

You discovered that a chemical reaction happens when you mix baking soda and vinegar together.

**1.** How do you know that a chemical reaction took place?

......................................................................................................................

......................................................................................................................

......................................................................................................................

## A Classic Experiment: Part 2

You discovered that when you mix larger amounts of baking soda and vinegar together, you get a chemical reaction.

**2.** How was the chemical reaction in Part 2 different than in Part 1?

......................................................................................................................

......................................................................................................................

......................................................................................................................

## A Classic Experiment: Part 3

You discovered that adding less vinegar to a large amount of baking soda meant that some of the baking soda was left over at the end.

**3.** Do you think a chemical reaction still occured in Part 3?

　**A.** Yes

　**B.** No

**4.** Do you think the amounts of matter that are used as reactants matters in a chemical reaction?

　**A.** Yes

　**B.** No

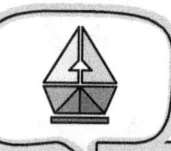
*You have spent a few days exploring chemical reactions. Today you will experiment further with more reactions that you can create in your own home.*

### Materials:

1. Vinegar
2. Salt
3. A small, shallow dish
4. Spoon
5. A handful of different coins, preferably ones that are dirty (older coins tend to be dirtier)
6. A hand towel

### Procedure:

1. Start by laying out all of the coins and observing them. Notice that the dirtier the coin is, the less shiny it is and the harder it is to see what is etched on it.
2. Now, try to clean a couple of the coins with a towel. Take a couple minutes to try this before moving on to the next step.
3. In the dish, mix $\frac{1}{4}$ cup of vinegar a tablespoon of salt. Mix this until most of the salt is totally dissolved.
4. Now place your coins in one layer on the bottom of the dish. They should not be touching each other or on top of each other.
5. Wait 5 minutes and then remove the coins from the dish and try to clean them with the towel. If they still seem dirty, you can place them back in the dish for another 5 minutes and then try again.

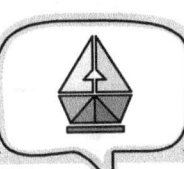
**Follow-up Questions:**

**1.** What are the reactants in the mixture that you made in the dish?

.................................................................................................................................

**2.** Was it hard to clean the coins with just the towel?

.................................................................................................................................

.................................................................................................................................

.................................................................................................................................

.................................................................................................................................

.................................................................................................................................

**3.** Why do you think it was important to use dirty coins in this experiment?

.................................................................................................................................

.................................................................................................................................

.................................................................................................................................

.................................................................................................................................

**4.** When you tried to clean the coins after leaving them in the salt in vinegar, what happened?

.................................................................................

.................................................................................

.................................................................................

.................................................................................

.................................................................................

.................................................................................

.................................................................................

.................................................................................

*Yesterday, you experimented with the chemical reaction of a salt and vinegar mixture and saw how it could be used to clean coins. Today you will elaborate on your observations.*

**Directions:** Read and answer each question below.

1. What was the product in this experiment?

................................................................................................................

................................................................................................................

................................................................................................................

2. Do you think the chemical reaction that helped clean the pennies would occur if you used just vinegar or just salt?

................................................................................................................

................................................................................................................

................................................................................................................

3. If you left the coins in there for a whole hour, do you think it would be easier or harder to clean them?

................................................................................................................

................................................................................................................

................................................................................................................

4. Can you think of another chemical reaction in everyday life?

................................................................................................................

................................................................................................................

................................................................................................................

................................................................................................................

# WEEK 6

# Physical Science
## Food & Energy

5-PS3-1

Make observations to construct an evidence-based account about how energy from food is used by living organisms.

ARGOPREP

**Directions:** Read the text below. Then answer the questions that follow.

## Energy From Food

All animals on our planet need food in order to survive. You eat food throughout the day, including meals and snacks. If you have a pet, you need to provide food for them as well. You have likely seen animals outside eating things like grass, nuts, or even other animals. But why do animals eat? It is because animals require **energy**. Energy is the ability to do work. In animals, this work can include everything from growing, to repairing their bodies when they are sick or injured, to simply moving around every day. Without energy, animals cannot survive.

1. What do animals need in order to survive?

   A. Acorns

   B. A friend

   C. Energy

   D. Movement

2. What is the ability to do work called?

   A. Matter

   B. Energy

   C. Food

   D. Growth

3. Which of these does NOT require energy from food?

   A. A volcanic eruption

   B. Growing

   C. Moving

   D. Repairing an injury

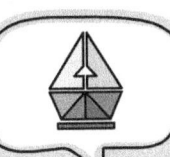
*Yesterday, you learned that animals need energy from food in order to do most things. Today you will explore the idea of energy in more detail.*

**Directions:** Read each text below and complete the activity. Then answer the questions that follow.

## Hunger & Energy

Take a moment to consider what it feels like to be hungry. Usually you are hungry when you haven't eaten in awhile. Sometimes this can make us feel tired or irritable.

**1.** When you are hungry, what does your body want more of?

A. Food

B. Energy

C. Both

## Pretty Pink Flamingos

Flamingos are a beautiful bird that feeds on shrimp from the ocean. Healthy flamingos eat a lot of shrimp and have bright pink feathers. Flamingos that are not healthy are not eating enough shrimp and usually have dull, less pink feathers.

**2.** If a flamingo is a really bright pink color, what is it eating a lot of?

## The Tallest Giraffe

A scientist is watching a herd of giraffes. He notices that one baby giraffe eats 4 times a day whereas another baby giraffe eats only 2 times a day. The giraffe that eats 4 times a day is about 8 feet tall whereas the giraffe that eats 2 times a day is 6 feet tall.

**3.** Which giraffe is taller?

A. The giraffe that eats 4 times a day

B. The giraffe that eats 2 times a day

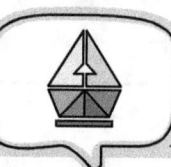
*Yesterday, you explored how food can be used as energy in animals. Today you will elaborate on the work energy does in the bodies of animals.*

**Directions:** Read each text below. Then answer the questions that follow.

## Hunger & Energy

You discovered that when you are hungry, your body wants food and energy.

**1.** Why does your body want both food and energy?

## Pretty Pink Flamingos

You discovered that healthy flamingos eat more shrimp and therefore have bright pink feathers.

**2.** What two things do flamingos use the energy from shrimp to do?

    **A.** Stay healthy

    **B.** Eat less

    **C.** Grow pink feathers

    **D.** Grow dull feathers

## The Tallest Giraffe

You discovered that a baby giraffe that eats more frequently throughout the day is taller.

**3.** What do baby giraffes use the energy from their food to do?

**4.** Do you think the shorter giraffe eats more or less energy than the taller giraffe?

    **A.** More

    **B.** Less

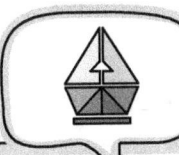
*You have spent a few days considering how the energy from food affects animals and how they use it in their bodies. Today you will experiment further with this concept.*

### Materials:

1. 5 different food items in their original packaging including:
   - **A.** Pasta
   - **B.** Candy bar
   - **C.** Milk
   - **D.** Beans (either dried or canned)
   - **E.** A type of frozen vegetable like peas or broccoli
2. A computer

### Procedure:

1. Lay the food out in front of you and locate the "Nutrition Facts" on the packaging. This is usually a black and white label that includes information like serving size, calories, and vitamins or minerals found in the food.
2. Write down how many calories are in a serving of each type of food in the table on the next page. This is usually found towards the top of the label. **Calories** are a measurement of how much energy is in the food.
3. Write down how big a serving size is for each type of food. This is also found towards the top of the packaging and is often in cups or number of pieces.
4. Write down whether or not you think each food type is "healthy" for you or not. Healthy things are generally good for you while unhealthy things aren't as good for you. If you are unsure, you can write that down.

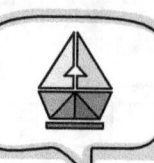
Data Table:

|  | Pasta | Candy Bar | Milk | Beans | Frozen Vegetable |
|---|---|---|---|---|---|
| **Calories** | | | | | |
| **Serving Size** | | | | | |
| **Is it healthy or not?** | | | | | |

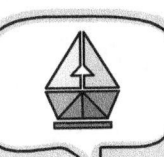
*Yesterday, you explored how much energy is in a serving size of different types of food. Today you will elaborate on the data that you collected.*

**Directions:** Read and answer each question below.

**1.** What food had the most calories in one serving?

.....................................................................................................

.....................................................................................................

**2.** What food had the biggest serving size?

.....................................................................................................

.....................................................................................................

**3.** Which food or foods do you think are healthiest? Why?

.....................................................................................................

.....................................................................................................

.....................................................................................................

.....................................................................................................

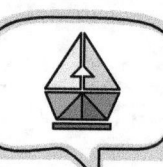
**4.** A candy bar is not very healthy. Does it have a lot of energy (calories) in it or not?

.................................................................................................................................

.................................................................................................................................

**5.** Do you think it is important to get your energy from only one type of food or many types of food? Why?

.................................................................................................................................

.................................................................................................................................

.................................................................................................................................

.................................................................................................................................

.................................................................................................................................

**6.** If you eat healthy foods with a lot of energy in them, what can that help you do?

.................................................................................................................................

.................................................................................................................................

.................................................................................................................................

.................................................................................................................................

.................................................................................................................................

.................................................................................................................................

.................................................................................................................................

# Life Science
## Plants & Energy

5-LS1-1

$C_6H_{12}O_6$

$O_2$

$CO_2$

$H_2O$

Make observations to construct an evidence-based account about how plants need air and water to grow.

ARGOPREP

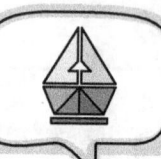
**Directions:** Read the text below. Then answer the questions that follow.

## Where Do Plants Get Their Energy From?

Plants are incredible organisms that have one of the most important jobs on Earth. Plants are the only organisms that can capture the sun's light energy and turn it into a different form of energy called sugar which all living organisms can use. This process is known as **photosynthesis**. Plants use carbon dioxide ($CO_2$) and water ($H_2O$) from the environment and turn it into sugar ($C_6H_{12}O_6$) and oxygen ($O_2$) by using the power of the sun's light (energy). Below is the **equation** for the chemical reaction of photosynthesis. An equation tells us what goes into a reaction and what comes out of it. Review what you learned in Week 5 about the reactants and products of chemical reactions if you'd like to. Without the process of photosynthesis, all organisms on our planet would run out of energy and would not be able to survive.

1. Plants capture the sun's light energy to make energy in the form of sugar in a process known as

   A. Reactants

   B. Products

   C. Photosynthesis

   D. Equations

2. What two things do plants need in order to make sugar?

   A. Carbon dioxide and water

   B. Products and reactants

   C. Energy and oxygen

   D. Sunlight and equations

3. What tells us the things that go into a reaction and the things that come out of it?

   A. Plants

   B. Photosynthesis

   C. Products

   D. Equations

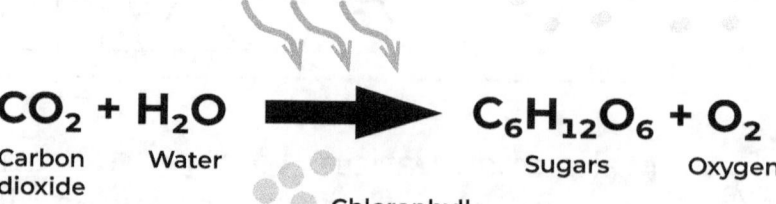

Sun's energy

$$CO_2 + H_2O \longrightarrow C_6H_{12}O_6 + O_2$$

Carbon dioxide — Water — Chlorophyll — Sugars — Oxygen

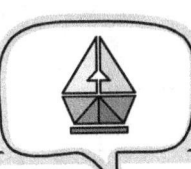
*Yesterday, you learned that plants need carbon dioxide and water in order to make sugar from the energy in sunlight. Today you will explore photosynthesis in your own home.*

**Directions:** Read each text below and complete the activity. Then answer the questions that follow.

## Celery Stalks

Take two stalks of celery and place one in a cup by itself and place the other in a cup that is half full of water. Place them on the countertop overnight and then observe them in the morning.

**1.** What do you think will happen to the celery with no water?

_____

_____

_____

_____

_____

_____

## The Shape Of Leaves

Go outside and observe a few different plants. Notice the shape of the leaves and where they are on the plant.

**2.** Draw a picture of one of the leaves you observed.

**3.** Are leaves thick like this workbook or thin like a single piece of paper?

   **A.** Thick

   **B.** Thin

## Who Turned The Light Off?

Take two seedlings or small plants that are very similar or even the same type of plant. Place one in a dark cupboard or closet, and place the other one on a sunny windowsill. Come back in a day or two and observe any differences.

**4.** What does the plant in the cupboard or closet not have access to that is necessary for the process of photosynthesis?

   **A.** Air

   **B.** Oxygen

   **C.** Carbon dioxide

   **D.** Light

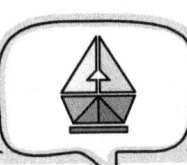
*Yesterday, you explored photosynthesis and plants in your own home. Today you will elaborate on your observations.*

**Directions:** Read each text below. Then answer the questions that follow.

## Celery Stalks

You discovered that celery that is left on a countertop with no water overnight will begin to wilt. Celery that has water stays pretty crisp however.

**1.** Why do you think the celery without any water wilted?

....................................................................................................................

....................................................................................................................

....................................................................................................................

....................................................................................................................

## The Shape Of Leaves

You discovered that leaves have many different shapes but they are always very thin and flat.

**2.** Why do you think leaves are thin and flat? Hint: leaves have the ability to capture the sun's light energy.

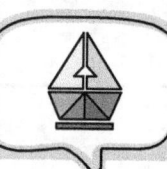
## Who Turned The Light Off?

You discovered that a plant with access to sunlight grows better than a plant with no access to sunlight.

**3.** Why do you think the plant without sunlight did not do very well? Hint: think about the process of photosynthesis and what it requires.

.................................................................................................

.................................................................................................

.................................................................................................

.................................................................................................

.................................................................................................

.................................................................................................

.................................................................................................

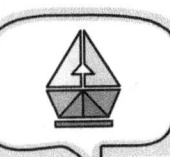
*You have spent the last couple of lessons learning about how photosynthesis works and what happens to plants when they don't have what they need to make energy and grow. Today you will explore photosynthesis in more detail.*

## Materials:

1. Water
2. Baking soda
3. A piece of aquatic plant such as Elodia, Ludwigia, Cabomba, or Stonewort. Any inexpensive aquatic plant will do and you can find them easily at pet or fish stores. You can also order them online.
4. A clear glass jar with a tight-fitting lid (like a mason jar) big enough to fit your plant

## Procedure:

1. Fill the glass jar about $\frac{4}{5}$ of the way with water.
2. Mix 2 tablespoons of baking soda into the water - baking soda releases carbon dioxide when it mixes with water.
3. Place your plant inside the jar and close the lid. The majority of the plant should be completely submerged in water - it's okay if a little bit sticks out.
4. Place the jar in a sunny place for 15 - 20 minutes and then observe your jar. Pay close attention to what you see on the leaves of the plant now.

### Follow-Up Questions

1. When your aquatic plant is making energy, what process is it doing?

2. Why did you place the jar in a sunny place?

3. What formed on the leaves of the plant after 15-20 minutes?

4. What do you think was in the tiny bubbles that formed on the leaves?

*Yesterday, you experimented with an aquatic plant and watched it create tiny bubbles while it did the process of photosynthesis. Today you will elaborate on your observations.*

**Directions:** Read and answer each question below.

**1.** Why did you need to submerge your aquatic plant in water?

.......................................................................................................................................

.......................................................................................................................................

.......................................................................................................................................

.......................................................................................................................................

**2.** Why did you need to mix baking soda into the water? What did it provide for the plant?

.......................................................................................................................................

.......................................................................................................................................

.......................................................................................................................................

.......................................................................................................................................

**3.** If you placed your jar in a dark closet, do you think your experiment would have worked?

.......................................................................................................................................

.......................................................................................................................................

.......................................................................................................................................

.......................................................................................................................................

**4.** Why can't you see the oxygen that trees make during photosynthesis but you could see the oxygen that your aquatic plant made?

.......................................................................................................................................

.......................................................................................................................................

.......................................................................................................................................

.......................................................................................................................................

# Life Science

## Types Of Consumers

5-LS2-1

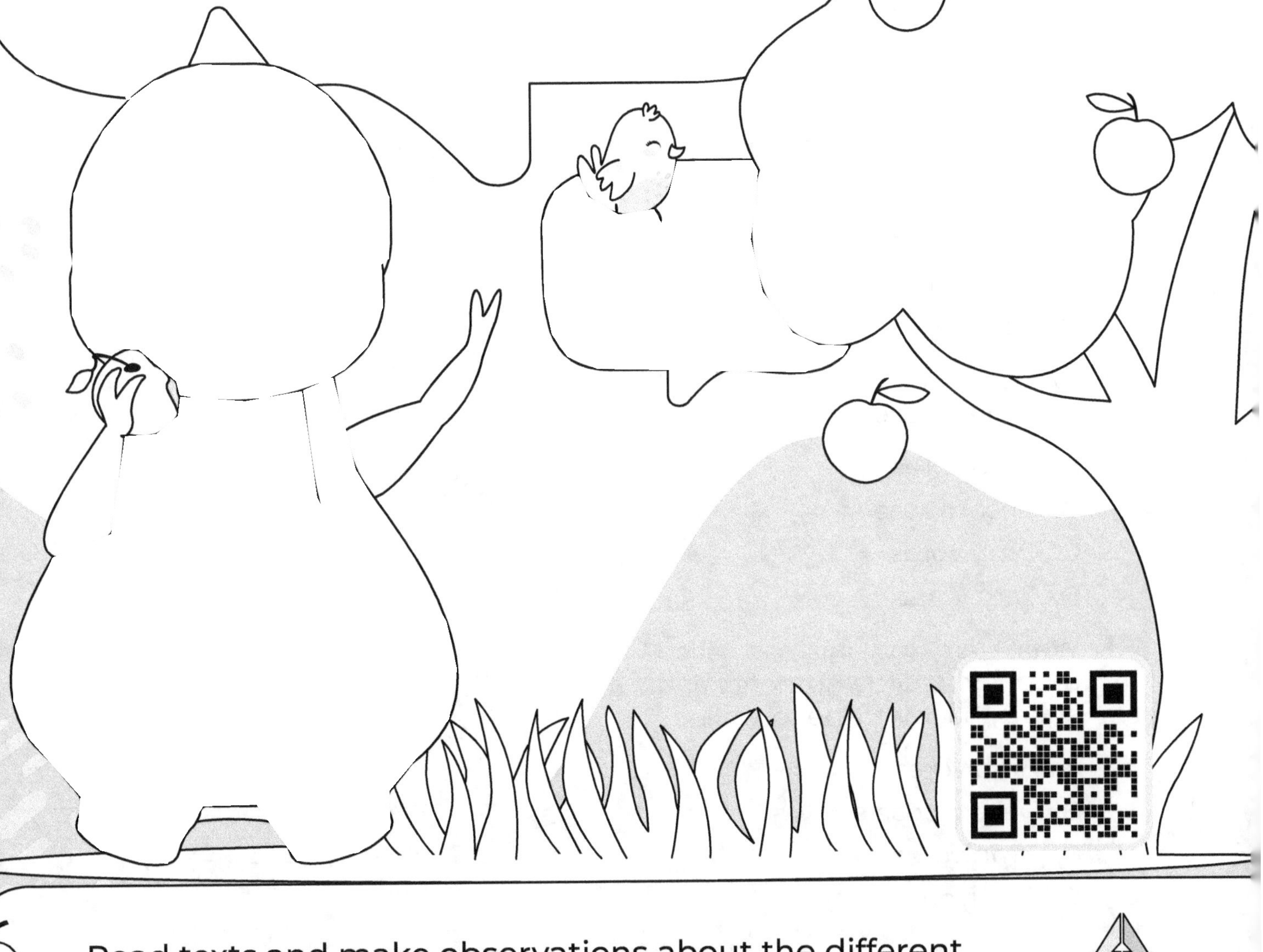

Read texts and make observations about the different types of consumers in various ecosystems.

**Directions:** Read the text below. Then answer the questions that follow.

## Who Eats What?

You learned last week that all animals eat food and that food provides energy. But not all animals eat the same types of food. Organisms that eat other organisms in order to get their energy are called **consumers**. Consumers can have lots of different types of diets. Animals like cows are known as **herbivores** because they only eat plants such as grass. Animals like lions are known as **carnivores** because they only eat meat. And animals like bears are known as **omnivores** because they eat both plants and animals. Animals like worms which eat dead organisms are known as **decomposers** - worms help recycle important nutrients and energy back into the soil.

1. What are organisms that eat other organisms called?

   A. Herbivores

   B. Decomposers

   C. Omnivores

   D. Consumers

2. What are organisms that eat only meat called?

   A. Herbivores

   B. Decomposers

   C. Omnivores

   D. Carnivores

3. What are organisms called that help recycle nutrients and energy back into the soil called?

   A. Herbivores

   B. Decomposers

   C. Omnivores

   D. Carnivores

*Yesterday, you learned that different animals eat different kinds of things. Today you will read about a few cool animals and identify what kind of consumer they are.*

**Directions:** Read each text below and complete the activity. Then answer the question that follows.

### Hiding Their Bounty

Squirrels are known for finding and hiding food throughout the warmer months to eat during the winter. They store things like seeds, nuts, and small pieces of plants.

**1.** Based on what you read, what type of consumer do you think squirrels are?

   **A.** Carnivores

   **B.** Herbivores

   **C.** Omnivores

   **D.** Decomposers

### Beautiful Bowerbirds

Bowerbirds are a type of bird that build very beautiful shelters to live in and to attract mates. They tend to decorate their nests with really beautiful colors. Most bowerbirds eat things like grasshoppers, flowers, and worms.

**2.** Based on what you read, what type of consumer do you think bowerbirds are?

   **A.** Carnivores

   **B.** Herbivores

   **C.** Omnivores

   **D.** Decomposers

### A Very Helpful Fungi

Winter Fungus is a type of mushroom that grows on dead tree trunks and breaks them down in order to use their energy and nutrients. This mushroom is a bright orange color and grows throughout the year, even in colder months.

**3.** Based on what you read, what type of consumer do you think winter fungus is?

   **A.** Carnivores

   **B.** Herbivores

   **C.** Omnivores

   **D.** Decomposers

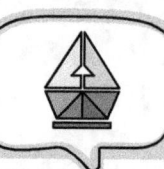
*Yesterday, you explored different types of consumers in the world and what they eat. Today you will elaborate on your findings.*

**Directions:** Read each text below. Then answer the questions that follow.

## Hiding Their Bounty

You discovered that squirrels are considered herbivores.

**1.** What types of foods do squirrels consume that let you know they are herbivores?

....................................................................................

....................................................................................

....................................................................................

## Beautiful Bowerbirds

You discovered that bowerbirds are considered omnivores.

**2.** What types of foods do bowerbirds consume that let you know they are omnivores?

....................................................................................

....................................................................................

....................................................................................

....................................................................................

## A Very Helpful Fungi

You discovered that winter fungi are considered decomposers.

**3.** What types of foods do winter fungi consume that let you know they are decomposers?

....................................................................................

....................................................................................

....................................................................................

....................................................................................

*You have spent the last couple of lessons learning about the different types of consumers and their diets. Today you will explore different types of consumers in a specific ecosystem.*

### Materials:

1. Computer or library for research.

### Background Information:

The Papua Rainforest in Papua New Guinea is considered to be one of the most diverse ecosystems in the world. There are more types of plants, animals, fungi and bacteria in these rainforests than anywhere else on the planet! Some very interesting and beautiful consumers are native to these rainforests and can only be found in Papua New Guinea. Today, research some of the species of animals listed below and determine what type of consumer they are based on your research. Fill in the table as you read about these fascinating creatures.

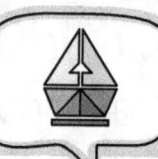
**Data Table:**

| Animal | Types of Foods It Eats | What Type Of Consumer Is It? |
|---|---|---|
| **Tree Kangaroos** | | Omnivore |
| **King Bird of Paradise** | Fruit, Flowers, and Insects | |
| **Long-Beaked Echidna** | Insects & Earthworms | |
| **Burying Beetle** | | Decomposer |
| **Blue Emperor Butterfly** | | Herbivore |

*Yesterday, you explored a few of the incredible consumers found in the rainforests of Papua New Guinea. Today you will answer some questions based on your research.*

**Directions:** Read and answer each question below.

1. Are there a lot of different types of diets that organisms in the rainforest have?

   **A.** Yes

   **B.** No

2. Would the Long-Beaked Echidna be more likely to eat a Burying Beetle or nuts from a tree? Why?

   _____

   _____

   _____

   _____

   _____

   _____

   _____

3. Why do Blue Emperor Butterflies rely on plants for energy? What is their main food source?

   _____

   _____

   _____

   _____

   _____

   _____

   _____

   _____

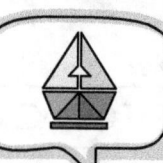
**4.** Which organism is important for recycling energy and nutrients back into the soil of the rainforest?

.................................................................................................................

**5.** What type of consumer are you? Which rainforest animal are you most like if you compare your diets?

.................................................................................................................
.................................................................................................................
.................................................................................................................
.................................................................................................................
.................................................................................................................
.................................................................................................................

# WEEK 9

# Life Science

## Food Webs

5-LS2-1

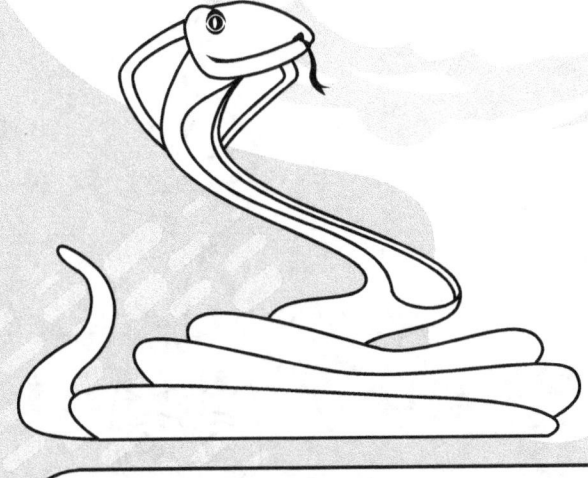

Make observations and gather information about how food chains and food webs are involved in the cycling of matter and energy.

ARGOPREP

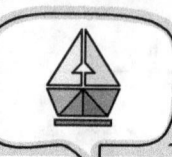
**Directions:** Read the text below. Then answer the questions that follow.

## Who Eats What?

So far you have learned how organisms get energy. Plants make their energy from the sun and consumers get their energy from eating other organisms. Today we will look at how energy moves around an ecosystem in what is called a **food chain**. A food chain shows what organisms eat other organisms for energy. Remember that plants are producers and make their energy directly from the sun so they don't need to eat other organisms to live and grow. Because of this, producers are always at the start of every food chain. Consumers that eat producers are called **primary consumers** because they are the first organisms to get energy from producers. **Secondary consumers** are organisms that eat primary consumers and sometimes plants too. **Tertiary consumers** eat secondary consumers and are at the end of the food chain.

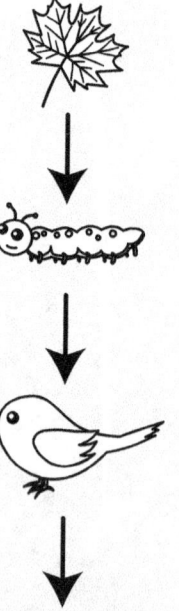

1. What is used to show how energy moves around an ecosystem?

   A. Producers
   B. Food Chain
   C. Consumers
   D. Photosynthesis

2. What types of consumers eat producers?

   A. Primary Consumers
   B. Secondary Consumers
   C. Plants
   D. Decomposers

3. What types of consumers eat other consumers?

   A. Primary Consumers
   B. Secondary Consumers
   C. Tertiary Consumers
   D. Both B & C

*Yesterday, you learned what types of organisms are found in food chains. Today you will explore how different types of diets can tell us where an organism might be in a food chain.*

**Directions:** Read each text below. Then answer the question that follows. Each question relates to the food chain pictured below.

## The Base Of The Food Chain

Carrots are the base of this food chain and pictured all the way on the left. Carrots are able to make their own food from the sun's energy, carbon dioxide, and water. Without carrots and other plants, the consumers in this ecosystem would be able to get the energy they need to survive.

1. Based on what you read, what phrase best describes the carrot's role in this food chain?

   A. Primary Consumer

   B. Secondary Consumer

   C. Producer

   D. Decomposer

## The Middle Of The Food Chain

Rabbits are pictured in the middle of the food chain. In this ecosystem, their main source of energy is carrots but they also eat things like small seeds and flowers.

**2.** Based on what you read, what phrase best describes the rabbit's role in this food chain?

    **A.** Primary Consumer

    **B.** Secondary Consumer

    **C.** Producer

    **D.** Plant

## The Top Of The Food Chain

The wolf is pictured at the top of the food chain all the way on the right. In this ecosystem, their main source of energy is rabbits but they also eat things like mice, deer, nuts, and berries.

**3.** Based on what you read, what phrase best describes the wolf's role in this food chain?

    **A.** Primary Consumer

    **B.** Secondary Consumer

    **C.** Producer

    **D.** Herbivore

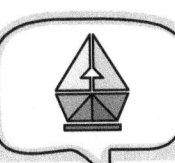
*Yesterday, you explored a food chain and learned about the roles of different organisms in a particular ecosystem. Today you will explain how their diets relate to what type of organism they are. You may want to look back at Week 8 to review the different types of consumers.*

**Directions:** Read each text below. Then answer the questions that follow.

### The Base Of The Food Chain

You discovered that carrots are producers at the base of a food chain.

**1.** In order for carrots to grow, what is one thing they need to make energy?

### The Middle Of The Food Chain

You discovered that rabbits are primary consumers in this ecosystem and are found in the middle of the food chain.

**2.** Based on what the rabbit eats, what type of consumer is it? You might want to re-read about the rabbit from yesterday's lesson and look back at Day 1 of Week 8 for help.

### The Top Of The Food Chain

You discovered that wolves are secondary consumers in this ecosystem and are found at the top of the food chain.

**3.** Based on what the wolf eats, what type of consumer is it? You might want to re-read about the wolf from yesterday's lesson and look back at Day 1 of Week 8 for help.

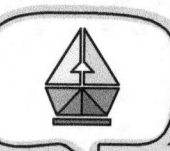
*Yesterday, you learned how different types of diets relate to where organisms might be found in a food chain. Today you will try to build your own food chain.*

### Background Information:

Plants and animals live both on land and in the water. Places like ponds, lakes, and the ocean that are home to organisms are known as **aquatic ecosystems.** Below are some organisms found together in a pond. Read the table below and then fill in the food chain so that the organisms are in the right order. The base of the food chain is on the left and the top of the food chain is on the right.

### Data Table:

| Organism | Description Of Organism | Types of Foods It Eats |
|---|---|---|
| **Mosquito Larvae** | The first stage of a mosquito's life before they develop wings for flying | Plants, algae, and water weed |
| **Algae** | A green aquatic organism that does photosynthesis | None |
| **Carp** | A large freshwater fish | Insect larvae, smaller fish, and plankton |
| **Kingfisher** | A beautiful blue bird known for its ability to dive into water to catch prey | Frogs, snakes, and fish |

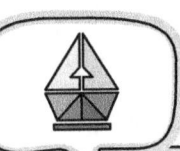
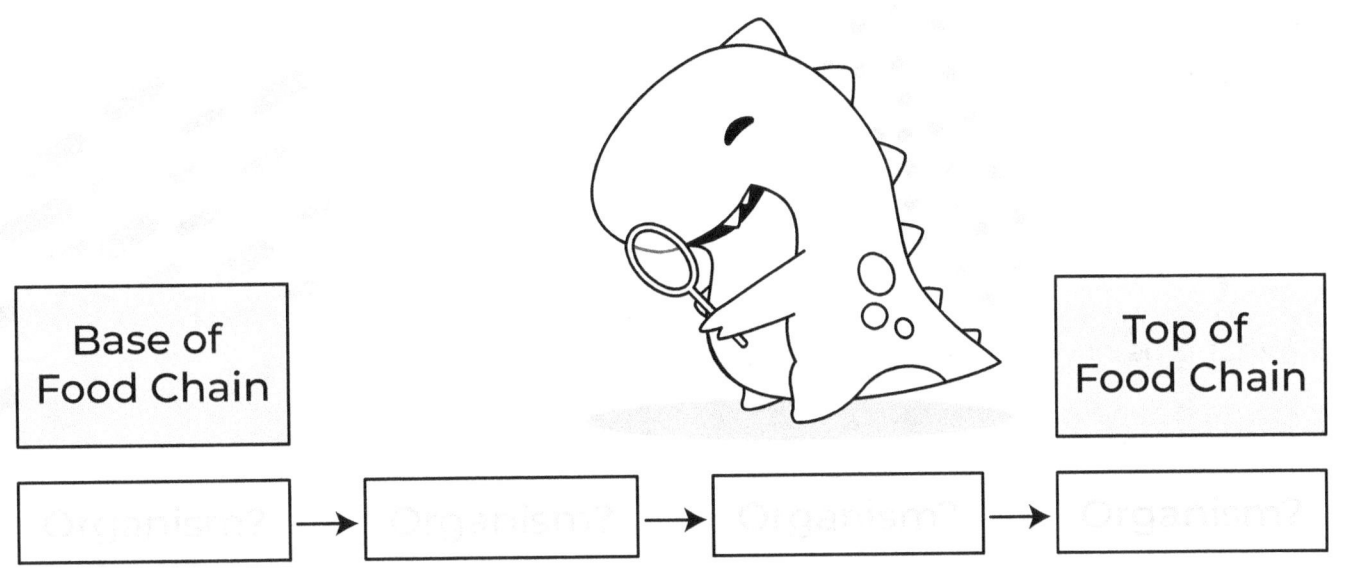

| Base of Food Chain | | Top of Food Chain |
|---|---|---|

| Organism? | → | Organism? | → | Organism? | → | Organism? |

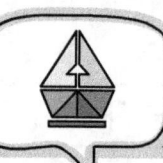
*Yesterday, you built your own food chain using information about the diets of different aquatic organisms. Today you will elaborate on this food chain.*

**Directions:** Read and answer each question below.

**1.** Why is the algae at the base of the food chain?

...................................................................................................

...................................................................................................

**2.** What type of consumer is the mosquito larvae?

   **A.** Primary

   **B.** Secondary

   **C.** Tertiary

**3.** What type of consumer is the carp?

   **A.** Primary

   **B.** Secondary

   **C.** Tertiary

**4.** What type of consumer is the kingfisher?

   **A.** Primary

   **B.** Secondary

   **C.** Tertiary

**5.** What type of diet do kingfishers have?

   **A.** Herbivore

   **B.** Carnivore

   **C.** Omnivore

   **D.** Decomposer

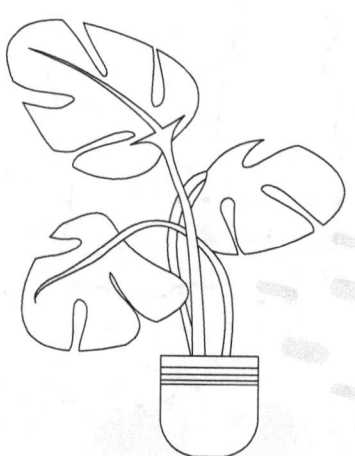

# Life Science

## Recycling Matter & Energy

5-LS2-1

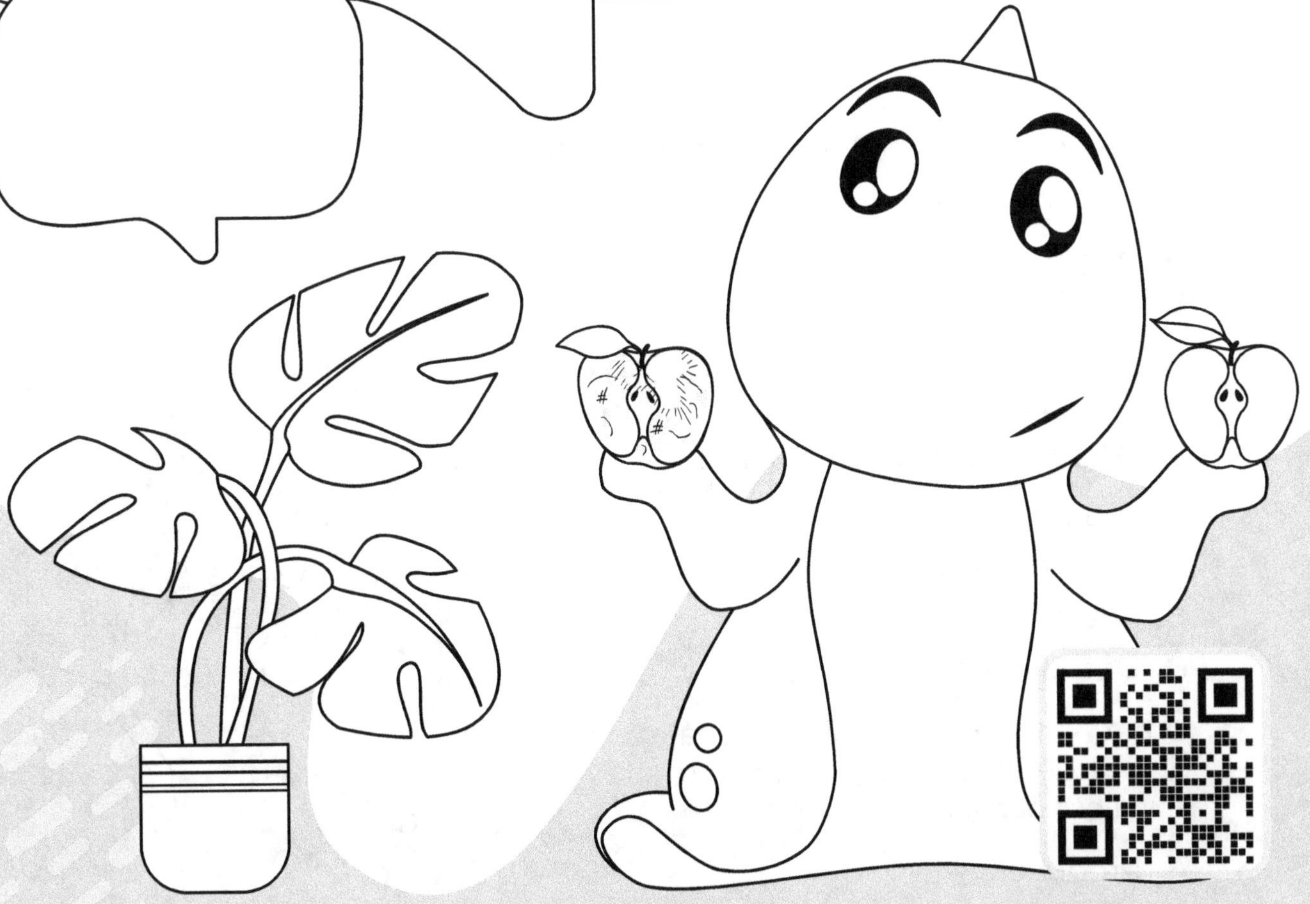

Make observations and gather information about the importance of decomposers and their role in recycling matter back into ecosystems.

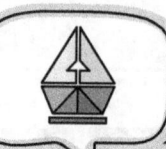
**Directions:** Read the text below. Then answer the questions that follow.

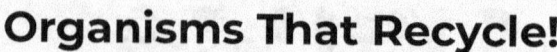

## Organisms That Recycle!

In a previous lesson you learned that **decomposers** are a type of consumer that breaks down dead organisms. This is so important because this allows energy and nutrients to be recycled back into the environment. Decomposers can be fungi, insects, worms, and even bacteria. **Scavengers** are organisms that are usually larger than decomposers and eat things like dead carcasses of animals. Scavengers include animals like racoons, coyotes, and vultures and their waste becomes food for decomposers. There are also organisms called **detritivores**. These organisms take the large particles that decomposers have broken down and break them down into smaller particles. For example, if a decomposer such a snail breaks down a leaf into large particles, a detritivore such as a pillbug would break those molecules down into smaller particles.

1. What type of large animals feed on animal carcasses?

   A. Decomposers

   B. Scavengers

   C. Detritivores

   D. Fungi

2. Fungi, worms, and insects are usually considered to be what?

   A. Producers

   B. Decomposers

   C. Scavengers

   D. Detritivores

3. What type of organism breaks down dead organisms into the smallest particles?

   A. Producers

   B. Decomposers

   C. Scavengers

   D. Detritivores

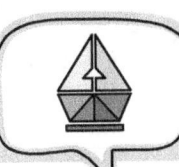
*Yesterday, you learned about the different kinds of organisms that recycle energy and nutrients. Today you will explore their importance in the ecosystem.*

**Directions:** Read each text below and complete the activity. Then answer the questions that follow.

## Leaves, Leaves Everywhere

Go outside and notice any plants around you. Now, pick up any leaves, sticks, or pieces of plants that are dead or are not attached to a plant any more. Observe them.

1. Do you think these pieces of plants are alive or dead?

   A. Alive

   B. Dead

2. Describe how they look compared to pieces of plants, such as leaves, that are still attached to the plant they come from.

   .................................................................................................................................

   .................................................................................................................................

   .................................................................................................................................

   .................................................................................................................................

   .................................................................................................................................

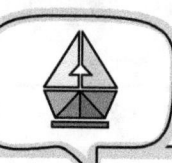
## Kitchen Recycling

Go online and research "composting" or "kitchen composting." Perhaps you have a compost at your own home.

**3.** What is composting?

    **A.** Throwing things in the trash

    **B.** Recycling plastic bottles and aluminum cans

    **C.** Breaking down materials that were once alive

    **D.** Turning off your lights when you leave a room

**4.** What types of things can be composted?

.................................................................................................................

.................................................................................................................

.................................................................................................................

## What Happened To My Apple?

Take half of an apple and place it in a glass jar with a tablespoon of water. Observe what it looks like. Leave the top of the glass jar off of it. Leave it on the counter for up to a week. Observe it at the end of the week.

**5.** What did the apple look like at the end of the week?

.................................................................................................................

.................................................................................................................

.................................................................................................................

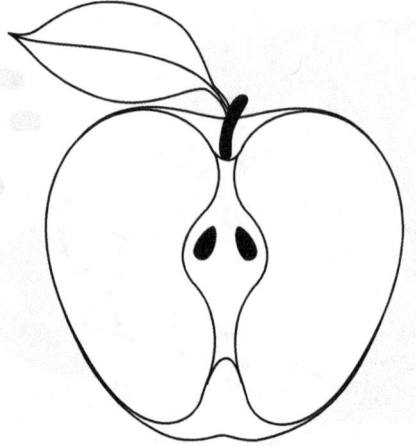
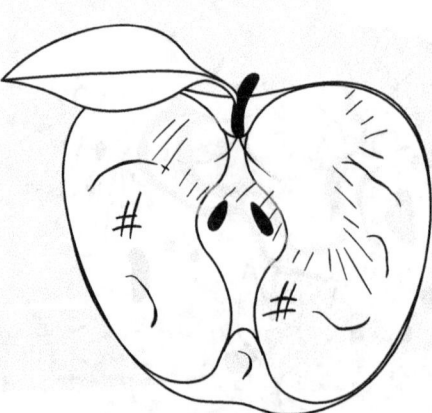

*Yesterday, you explored the different kinds of decomposers and how they break down different dead organisms in your environment. Today you will explain what you saw in these activities.*

**Directions:** Read each text below. Then answer the questions that follow.

### Leaves, Leaves Everywhere

You discovered that pieces of plants that are no longer attached to plants are dead and begin to become brown, dry, wrinkled, or brittle as they break down.

1. What types of organisms might be causing pieces of plants to break down?

   A. Decomposers

   B. Detritivores

   C. Scavengers

   D. A & B are both possible

### Kitchen Recycling

You discovered that composting helps break down things that were once alive such as vegetable scraps, leaves, and other dead organisms.

2. If you added earthworms or bacteria to an outdoor compost pile, what might happen?

   A. Your compost pile would begin to stink.

   B. Your compost pile would break down faster thanks to these decomposers.

   C. Your compost pile would not change at all.

### What Happened To My Apple

You discovered that a black, fuzzy mold (a type of fungus) will grow on an apple and begin to break it down.

3. Mold is not considered to be a scavenger. Why is that?

........................................................................................

........................................................................................

........................................................................................

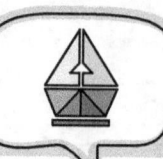
*Yesterday you explained how different types of organisms help recycle energy and nutrients back into the environment. Today you will experiment with a single decomposer known as yeast.*

## Background Information:

Yeast is a tiny, single-celled fungi that is used in baking. Yeast is good at breaking down the sugars in things like flour, fruit, and many vegetables and uses some of that energy to grow and make more yeast. Today you will experiment and see how yeast can break down the sugar in a banana very quickly!

## Materials:

1. Banana
2. Water
3. Packet of yeast
4. 2 plastic sandwich bags
5. Cutting board
6. Knife

## Procedure:

1. Peel your banana and cut it into 10 equal slices.
2. Place 5 slices in one flat layer inside the sandwich bag. Do the same with the other 5 slices in the other sandwich bag.
3. Sprinkle 1 teaspoon of water in each of the sandwich bags on top of the bananas.
4. Sprinkle 2 teaspoons of yeast on top of the bananas in only <u>one</u> of the bags.
5. Close the bags and leave them on a sunny countertop for 4 - 6 hours. Come back every hour and observe each of the bags without moving them - just observe with your eyes.

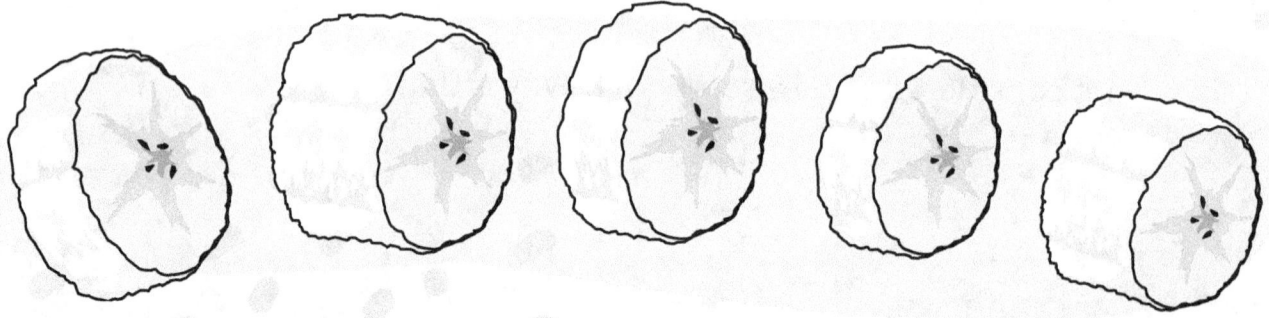

**Follow-up Questions:**

**1.** What type of organisms are yeast?

................................................................................................................

**2.** Are yeast decomposers, detritivores, or scavengers?

    **A.** Decomposer

    **B.** Detritivore

    **C.** Scavenger

**3.** What does the banana provide for the yeast?

................................................................................................................

**4.** By the end of the experiment, what did the banana look like in the bag that did not have yeast?

................................................................................................................

................................................................................................................

................................................................................................................

**5.** By the end of the experiment, what did the banana look like in the bag that also had yeast?

................................................................................................................

................................................................................................................

................................................................................................................

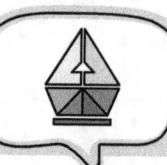
*Yesterday, you experimented with yeast and how it can decompose a banana. Today you will elaborate on your findings.*

**Directions:** Read and answer each question below.

1. Could you still see pieces of the banana in the bag with the yeast at the end of the experiment?

    **A.** Yes

    **B.** No

2. If you left the bananas in the bags for a few more days, do you think they would look different?

    _____

    _____

    _____

3. Do you think adding yeast to a compost pile would help things break down?

    _____

    _____

    _____

4. Do you think decomposers, detritivores, and scavengers are important? Why?

    _____

    _____

    _____

    _____

    _____

# WEEK 11

# Earth & Space Science

## The Sun

5-ESS1-1

Make observations to construct an evidence-based account about the relative distance between the Sun and Earth.

ARGOPREP

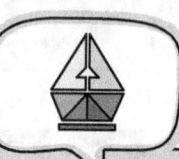
**Directions:** Read the text below. Then answer the questions that follow.

## The Brightest Star

**The Sun** is the biggest object in our solar system and plays an important role in how life gets energy, as we have seen in previous lessons. The Sun weighs 333,000 times more than Earth and is so big that all other planets orbit around it.

The Sun is a **star** because it is a hot ball of gases which glow and give us energy in the form of light and heat. When you look up at the sky, you can see thousands of stars which are a lot like the sun but they are in solar systems very far away. The reason our sun looks so much bigger than other stars is because it is so much closer to Earth. It would take us about 156 days to get to the Sun if we flew at 24,790 miles an hour. This is the fastest modern rockets can travel, but that is nothing compared to how long it would take us to get to the next closest star, **Alpha Centauri A**. If we wanted to get to Alpha Centauri A we would need to travel for at least 81,000 years at that same speed!

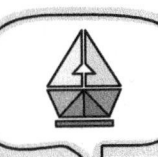
**1.** What is the biggest star in our solar system?

    **A.** Earth

    **B.** The Sun

    **C.** Alpha Centauri A

    **D.** Jupiter

**2.** How long would it take us to travel to the sun?

    **A.** 156 days

    **B.** 333,000 days

    **C.** 81,000 years

    **D.** 24,790 days

**3.** What is the name of the next closest star to Earth, not including the Sun?

    **A.** Alpha Centauri A

    **B.** The Sun

    **C.** Light Year

    **D.** Mercury

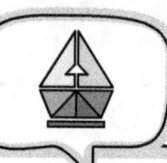
*Yesterday, you learned that the Sun is a star and that the sun looks so much bigger than other stars because it is very close to the Earth. Today you will explore this idea further.*

**Directions:** Read each text below and complete the activity. Then answer the question that follows.

## Tennis Balls, Near & Far

Take two tennis balls and place one of them 1 foot in front of you. Now walk away from that spot by taking 20 steps and then place the tennis ball where you end up. Make sure there is nothing blocking the way and that you can still see both tennis balls. Walk back to the original tennis ball. Compare how each of the tennis balls look.

**1.** Which tennis ball looks bigger?

    **A.** The closer tennis ball

    **B.** The further tennis ball

## Distance & Brightness

Make sure it is very dark or night time when you try this demo. Take two identical flashlights and place a piece of paper over the front of each one of the flashlights. You can hold it there with a rubber band. This is to diffuse the light so you can look at it without hurting your eyes. Similar to the last demo, place one flashlight facing you a foot in front of you and place the other flashlight 20 steps away. Make sure it is also facing you. Now observe how the light looks.

**2.** Which flashlight seems brighter?

    **A.** The closer flashlight

    **B.** The further flashlight

## Feel The Burn

Stand next to a heater or a vent in your home that is producing heat. Do not touch it, but notice that you can feel the warmth from it. Now take a few steps away from it and notice how the feeling of warmth changes. You can take a few more steps away again if you don't notice much change.

**3.** What happened to the feeling of warmth when you took a few steps away?

    **A.** It felt less warm.

    **B.** It felt more warm.

*Yesterday, you explored how the same thing can look and feel different when you are close to it compared to when you are far away from it. Today you will explain these phenomena.*

**Directions:** Read each text below. Then answer the questions that follow.

### Tennis Balls, Near & Far

You discovered that a tennis ball that is far away looks smaller than a tennis ball that is close to you.

**1.** If the sun was much further away from Earth, how might it look to you in terms of size?

### Distance & Brightness

You discovered that a flashlight that is far away from you does not seem to be as bright as a flashlight that is closer to you.

**2.** If the sun was much further away from Earth, how might it look to you in terms of brightness?

### Feel The Burn

You discovered that when you walk away from a heater, you cannot feel the warmth coming from it as much.

**3.** If the sun was much further away from Earth, how might the temperature on Earth be affected?

**4.** Do you think we can feel the heat coming from Alpha Centauri A, our closest neighboring star?

A. Yes

B. No

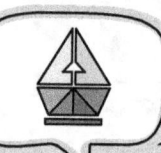
*Yesterday, you explained why the sun looks so much bigger and brighter than other stars in the universe. Today you will experiment with this idea by analyzing data.*

### Background Information:

Ollie buys a really nice telescope camera for looking at the stars and taking pictures. After taking some pictures, he notices that some of the stars look really big and some of the stars look really small. He wants to know if the size of the stars in his picture have anything to do with how far away they are from Earth. He is able to identify a few of the stars with the help of some star maps and his knowledge of the constellations.

### Procedure:

1. Look at the data table. It lists a few of the stars that Ollie was able to identify. Then look at the diameter of each star on the picture Ollie took. (The diameter is how wide across each star was.)

2. Use a computer and fill out how far away the stars are from Earth. This is usually reported in light years (LY). A light year is the distance you would travel if you were going the speed of light. Light moves very quickly, so a light year is a very long distance. Alpha Centauri A is already filled out for you.

Table:

| Name Of Star | Diameter Of Star On Photo | Distance From Earth (in light years) |
|---|---|---|
| Alpha Centauri A | 11 millimeters | 4.37 LY |
| Barnard's Star | 9 millimeters | |
| Luhman 16 | 6 millimeters | |
| Sirius | 3 millimeters | |

Follow-up Questions:

**1.** Which star is farthest from Earth?

.................................................................................................................................

**2.** What is the diameter of Luhman 16 in Ollie's photograph?

.................................................................................................................................

**3.** Which stars are more than 6 light years away?

.................................................................................................................................

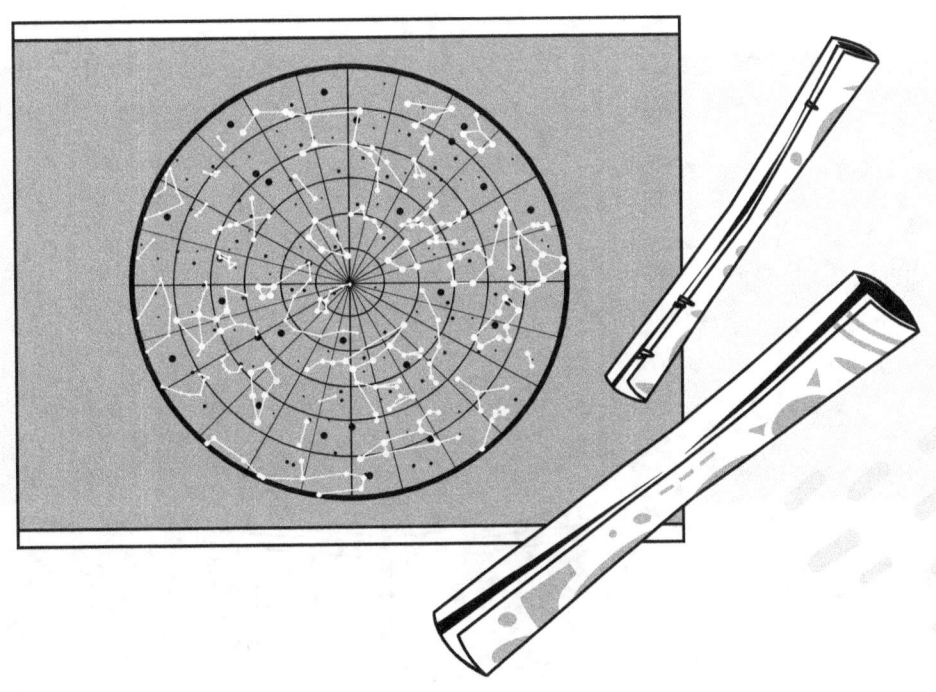

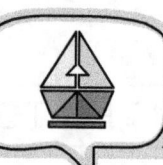
*Yesterday, you explored the distance of stars from Earth, specifically ones we can see in our constellations and take pictures using a telescope camera. Today you will elaborate on your findings and data.*

**Directions:** Read and answer each question below.

1.  When the distance from a star is further away from Earth, it will look _____ in a picture?

    **A.** Larger than other stars

    **B.** Smaller than other stars

    **C.** The same as all other stars

2.  If Ollie took a picture of the sun with this telescope camera, what might it look like?

    ................................................................

    ................................................................

3.  If Ollie took a picture of Wolf 359, a star that is 7.86 light years away, what other star from the data table might it look similar to in size?

    **A.** Sirius

    **B.** Luhman 16

    **C.** Alpha Centauri A

    **D.** Barnard's Star

4.  Which star from the data table would look the least bright in Ollie's picture?

    **A.** Sirius

    **B.** Luhman 16

    **C.** Alpha Centauri A

    **D.** Barnard's Star

# Earth & Space Science

## The Seasons

5-ESS1-2

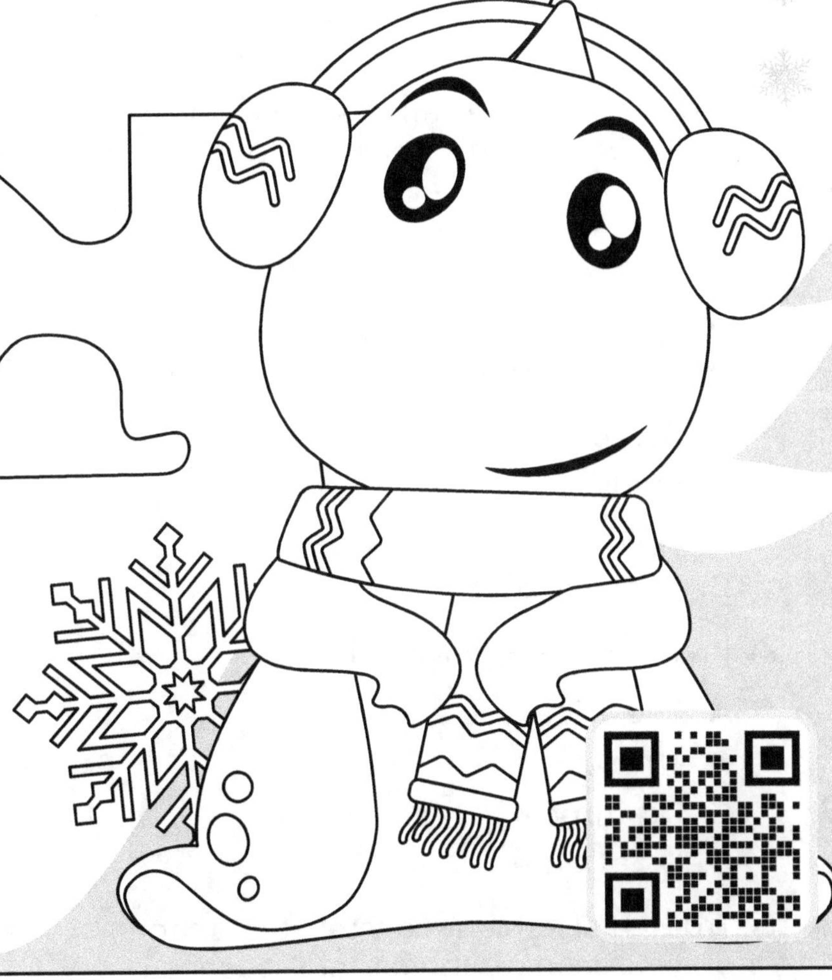

Make observations and analyze data about the different seasons and how the Sun impacts them.

ARGOPREP

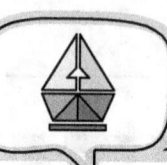
**Directions:** Read the text below. Then answer the questions that follow.

## Signs Of The Seasons

You no doubt have heard of the four seasons before - spring, summer, fall, and winter. You can see changes in your environment based on what season it is, even if you live in an area that doesn't have very drastic changes. There are a few telltale signs that you can notice about seasons, regardless of where you are in the world.

The Earth tilts towards the Sun on its **axis** at different angles throughout the year. The axis is sort of like a seesaw that Earth balances on - depending how Earth is angled on its axis, the length of day time and night time changes. In the winter, we get less day time and more night time because of the way Earth is tilted on its axis. This also makes the temperatures colder than in the summer months. The summer season has the longest day time and shortest night time, making these months warmer.

Earth's angle also affects what stars we can see during different seasons. Many constellations are only viewable during certain seasons because of Earth's tilt on its axis.

1. What acts like a seesaw and determines the angle at which Earth faces the sun?

   A. Seasons

   B. Signs

   C. Axis

   D. Constellations

2. In the summer, what is longer?

   A. The axis

   B. The season

   C. Day time

   D. Night time

3. True or False: Many constellations can only be seen during certain seasons.

   A. True

   B. False

*Yesterday, you learned that the seasons and stars change throughout the year because of how Earth is tilted on its axis. Today you will explore these ideas further.*

**Directions:** Read each text below and complete the activity. Then answer the question that follows.

### A Heated Question

Take a large towel and bundle it up into a ball. Dunk it in some water so the whole thing is equally wet - you may want to wring it out so that it is wet but not so much that it is dripping water everywhere. Take a blow dryer and begin to blowdry the towel from about 6 inches away on low heat. Hold the blow dryer in the exact same spot without moving it around. After 2-3 minutes turn off the blow dryer and feel the towel.

**1.** Where is the towel driest or warmest?

    **A.** In the area that the blow dryer was right above

    **B.** In the area that the blow dryer was not right above

    **C.** The whole towel is dry

### Right In Front Of Your Face

Take a paper map and hold it just in front of your face, a few inches from your nose. See how many things you can read or notice on the map. Now, move it a few inches in one direction and notice any new or different things you can see.

**2.** When you moved the map a few inches in a different direction, could you see different things?

    **A.** Yes                                 **B.** No

### Summertime Flashlight

Take a piece of aluminum foil and place it on a counter. Take a flashlight and hold it directly over the aluminum foil so that it is almost touching. Turn it on and hold it there for 20 seconds. Turn the flashlight off and then touch the aluminum foil, noticing its temperature. Turn the flashlight on again and hold it there for 1 minute. Turn the flashlight off and then touch the aluminum foil, noticing its temperature. If the temperature does not seem to have changed, try keeping the flashlight on for longer.

**3.** Did the aluminum get hotter the longer the flashlight was turned on above it?

    **A.** Yes                                 **B.** No

*Yesterday, you explored how the same thing can look and feel different when you are close to it compared to when you are far away from it. Today you will explain these phenomena.*

**Directions:** Read each text below. Then answer the questions that follow.

## A Heated Question

You discovered that a part of a towel dried quickest when a blowdryer was held directly above that spot.

**1.** If a place on the Earth is pointed at an angle directly towards the sun, what would the temperature be on that part of Earth?

   **A.** Hot

   **B.** Cold

**2.** What season would it likely be on that part of the planet?

   **A.** Winter

   **B.** Summer

## Right In Front Of Your Face

You discovered when you move a map in front of your face, you can see different things when you move it.

**3.** Pretend your eyes represent Earth on its axis in this activity. What did the map represent?

   **A.** The seasons

   **B.** The Sun

   **C.** Stars & Constellations

## Summertime Flashlight

You discovered aluminum foil will get warmer the longer a flashlight is turned on and held above the foil.

4. If the aluminum foil represented Earth, and the flashlight represented sun's light and heat, what did the length of time the flashlight was turned on represent?

   A. All of the seasons

   B. Day time

   C. Night time

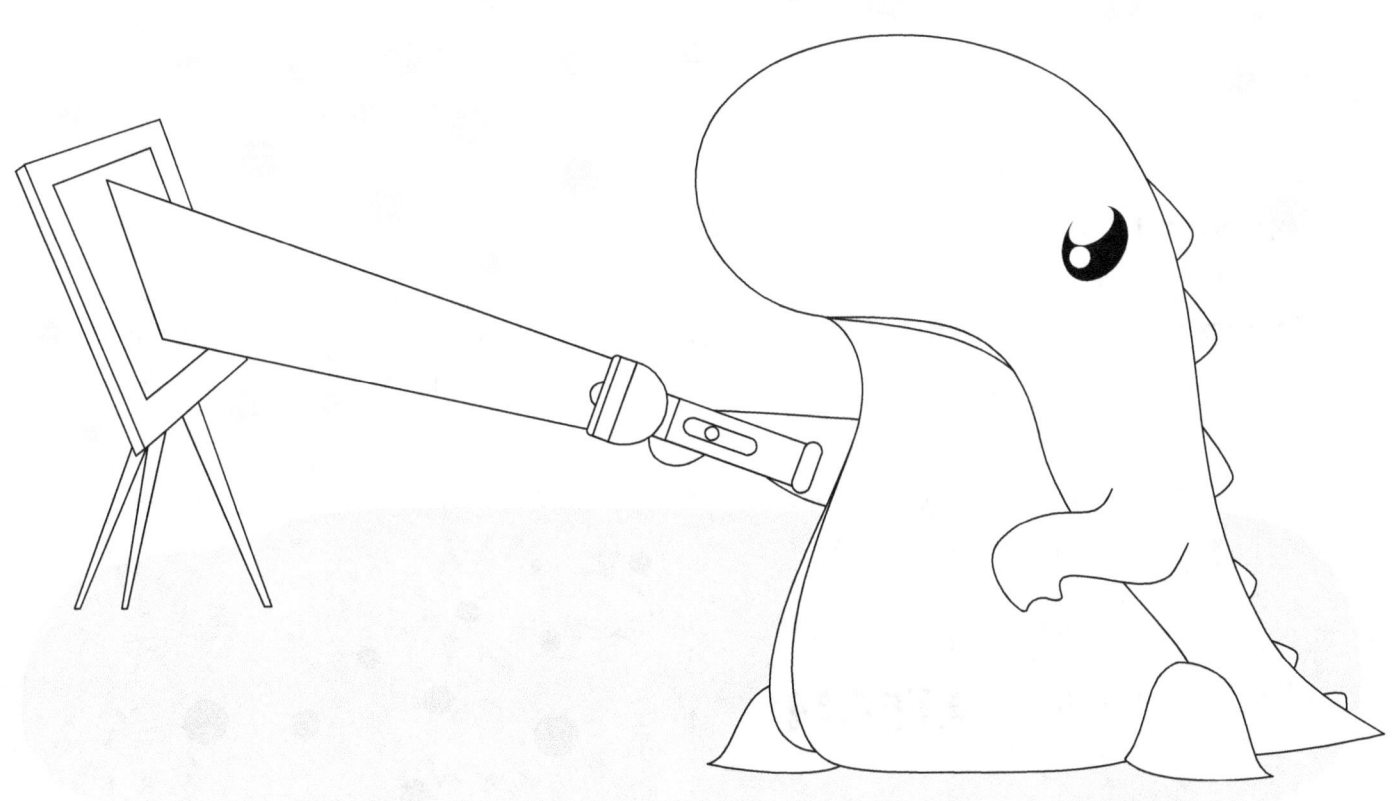

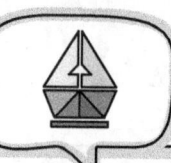
*Yesterday, you explored how heat and constellations can be impacted by the tilt of Earth on its axis during different seasons. Today you will analyze data about temperature, light, and constellations in one part of the United States throughout the year.*

### Background Information:

Below is a table that shows the average temperature, length of day time, length of night time, and number of constellations viewable in the state of Utah throughout the year. Analyze the data given and then answer the follow-up questions.

### Data Table:

| Month | Average Temperature | Length of Day | Length of Night | Number of Constellations |
|---|---|---|---|---|
| January | 37°F | 10 | 14 | 18 |
| February | 43°F | 10 | 14 | 18 |
| March | 53°F | 11 | 13 | 17 |
| April | 60°F | 11 | 13 | 19 |
| May | 70°F | 12 | 12 | 19 |
| June | 82°F | 12 | 12 | 17 |
| July | 90°F | 13 | 11 | 16 |
| August | 88°F | 13 | 11 | 19 |
| September | 77°F | 12 | 12 | 18 |
| October | 64°F | 12 | 12 | 19 |
| November | 48°F | 11 | 13 | 19 |
| December | 58°F | 10 | 14 | 17 |

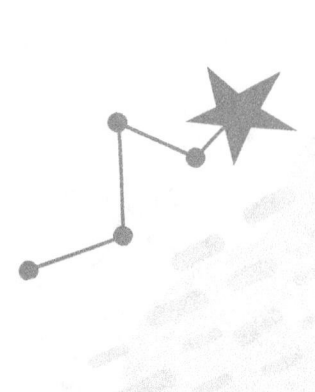

UTAH

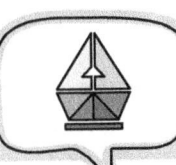
**Follow-up Questions:**

1. During what month does Utah experience the highest average temperature?

2. During what months does Utah experience the longest nights?

3. What is the fewest number of constellations you can see in Utah throughout the year?

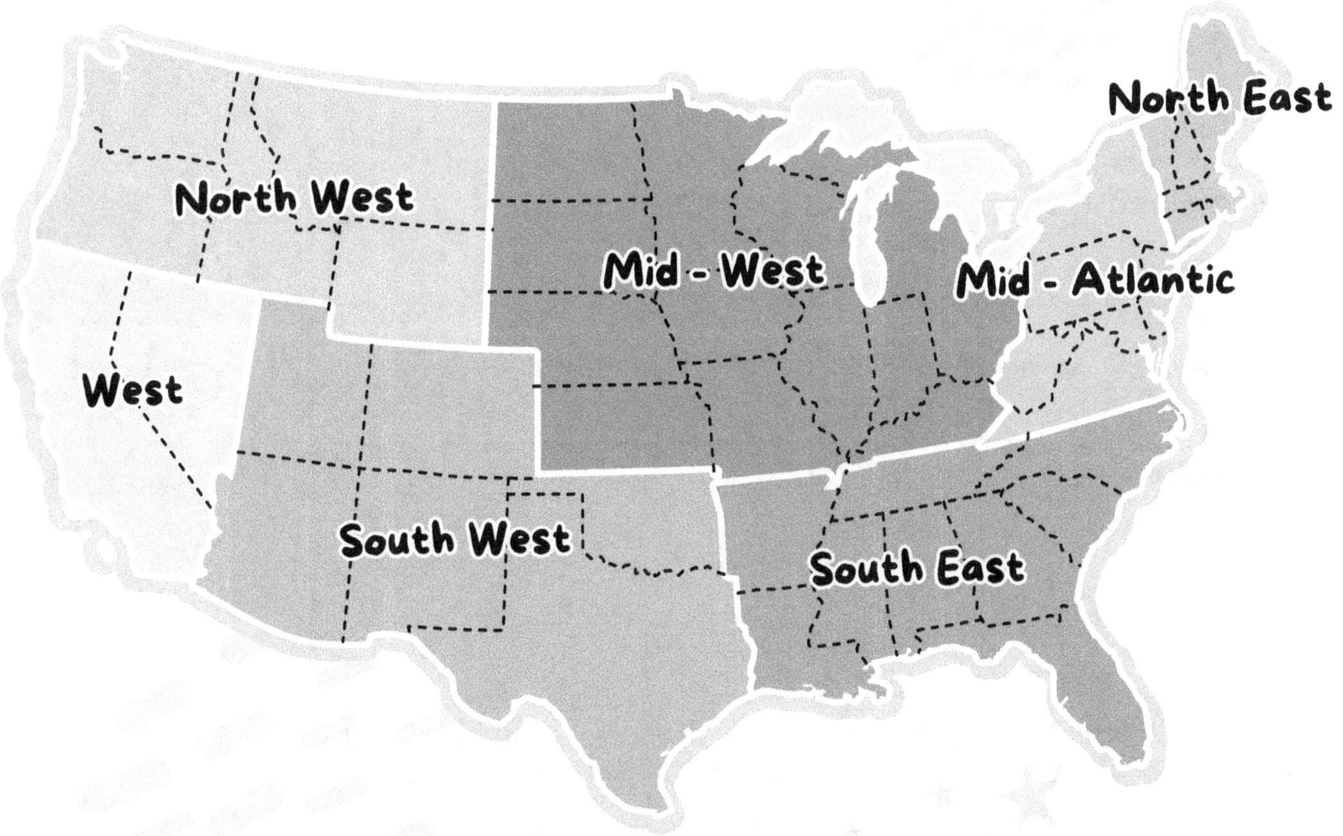

North East

North West

Mid - West

Mid - Atlantic

West

South West

South East

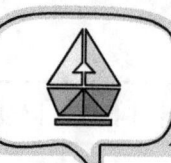
*Yesterday, you explored the data from Utah that relates to temperature, length of day, and number of constellations that can be seen throughout the year. Today you will elaborate on your findings.*

**Directions:** Read and answer each question below.

1. What do you notice about the temperature and length of day in the month of July?

......................................................................................................................

......................................................................................................................

......................................................................................................................

2. What is the length of night in the month of January? What is the average temperature that month?

......................................................................................................................

......................................................................................................................

......................................................................................................................

3. As the length of day increases, what happens to the length of night time?

   A. Increases

   B. Decreases

   C. Stays the same

4. Why does the length of day and night change throughout the year? Hint: relate this back to the axis of the Earth.

......................................................................................................................

......................................................................................................................

......................................................................................................................

5. Do you think the 17 constellations that can be seen in June are the same 17 constellations you can see in December? Why or why not?

......................................................................................................................

......................................................................................................................

......................................................................................................................

Use tools and materials to design a model that shows how the different spheres on Earth interact.

ARGOPREP

**Directions:** Read the text below. Then answer the questions that follow.

## The Spheres Of Earth

Our Earth is broken into different kinds of **spheres**. Each sphere contains similar factors and objects which help with different types of processes. For example, the **biosphere** contains places on Earth where life can exist. The **atmosphere** contains all of the gases that surround and protect our planet and is mostly above the surface of the planet. The atmosphere is also responsible for our weather and climate. The **geosphere** contains all of the landforms, rocks, and layers that make up Earth. Last there is the **hydrosphere** which contains all of the lakes, rivers, oceans, and any other water on the planet. These spheres interact with each other and can influence change in each other.

1. What sphere contains all of the landforms, rocks, and layers on Earth?

    A. Biosphere

    B. Hydrosphere

    C. Geosphere

    D. Atmosphere

2. What sphere surrounds Earth and contains many gases which protect us?

    A. Biosphere

    B. Hydrosphere

    C. Geosphere

    D. Atmosphere

3. What sphere contains all of the living organisms on Earth?

    A. Biosphere

    B. Hydrosphere

    C. Geosphere

    D. Atmosphere

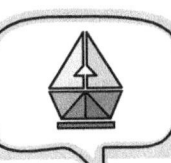
*Yesterday, you learned about the different spheres on Earth and that they can influence each other. Today you will explore these interactions in more detail.*

**Directions:** Read each text below and complete the activity. Then answer the questions that follow.

## Watering Your World

Go outside and water a few plants in your yard. If you do not have a yard, you can water an indoor plant. Remember that plants need sunlight and water in order to live and make their own energy. In this activity, you are acting like rain and bringing water to the plants.

**1.** What sphere is a plant part of?

**2.** What sphere is rain part of?

## A Sandy Situation

Go outside and make a small hill of sand, about 6 to 12 inches tall. Sit on one side of it and blow gently on the sand for a few breaths. Notice any changes. Now blow on the sand as hard as you can for a few breaths. Notice any changes that occur.

**3.** Did the sand change more when you blew on it gently or as hard as you could?

   **A.** Blew gently

   **B.** Blew hard as possible

## Life In & Around Water

If you have a stream or creek nearby, go ahead and visit it. If not, you can search for images of creeks and streams on the Internet. Notice all of the plants that live along the edge of a stream and even in it. Think about all of the animals that can live in a stream.

**4.** What is one animal that can live in or near a stream?

**5.** What is one plant that can live in or near a stream?

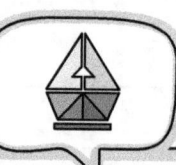
*Yesterday, you explored and modeled how different spheres on Earth can interact. Today you will explain your observations in more detail.*

**Directions:** Read each text below. Then answer the questions that follow.

## Watering Your World

You discovered that rain is a part of the atmosphere and that plants are a part of the biosphere.

**1.** Why is it important for the biosphere and the atmosphere to be able to interact? Think about the activity you did yesterday.

.............................................................................................................

.............................................................................................................

.............................................................................................................

.............................................................................................................

## A Sandy Situation

You discovered that a hill made of sand will change when you blow on it like the wind.

**2.** What sphere does wind belong to?

    **A.** Biosphere              **C.** Geosphere

    **B.** Hydrosphere         **D.** Atmosphere

**3.** What sphere does sand belong to?

    **A.** Biosphere              **C.** Geosphere

    **B.** Hydrosphere         **D.** Atmosphere

## Life In & Around Water

You discovered that living organisms like plants and animals live in and around creeks and streams.

**4.** Which two spheres are involved in this example?

    **A.** Biosphere/ Hydrosphere

    **B.** Hydrosphere/ Geosphere

    **C.** Geosphere/ Atmosphere

    **D.** Atmosphere/ Hydrosphere

*Yesterday, you explored how different spheres of the Earth can interact. Today you will experiment with these ideas in more detail by making a model that includes all of these spheres.*

## Materials:

1. A clear plastic box, similar in size to a shoebox (tupperware works well)
2. Sand & Dirt
3. Pebbles and small rocks
4. A few very small houseplants (succulents & shade plants work well)
5. A large water bottle filled with water.

## Procedure:

1. Start by putting a layer of pebbles on the bottom of your box, ½ to 1 inch thick.
2. Place a thicker layer of dirt on top of the pebble layer, making it uneven so that one side of the box has dirt almost to the top and the opposite side has only enough dirt to cover the pebbles just a little bit.
3. On the side with the thickest dirt, plant a couple of small houseplants.
4. Take your water bottle and gently pour a thin stream of water around the base of your house plants, keeping the bottle stationary in one spot. Keep pouring the water until the water bottle is empty. Extra water that is not absorbed by the dirt should collect in a pool somewhere in the box.

## Follow-up Questions:

1. What sphere does the dirt and rocks represent?

    A. Biosphere

    B. Hydrosphere

    C. Geosphere

    D. Atmosphere

2. What sphere do the house plants represent?

    A. Biosphere

    B. Hydrosphere

    C. Geosphere

    D. Atmosphere

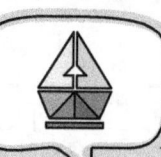
**3.** What sphere does the water coming out of the water bottle represent?

    **A.** Biosphere

    **B.** Hydrosphere

    **C.** Geosphere

    **D.** Atmosphere

**4.** What sphere does the water that collects in a pool in the box represent?

    **A.** Biosphere

    **B.** Hydrosphere

    **C.** Geosphere

    **D.** Atmosphere

*Yesterday, you made a model that included all of Earth's different spheres. Today you will elaborate on the interactions in your model between the spheres.*

**Directions:** Read and answer each question below.

1. When you poured the water, what did you notice about how the water moved down the dirt and into the pool of water?

   ........................................................................................

   ........................................................................................

2. An interaction between which two spheres was represented by creating a pool of water in your model?

   ........................................................................................

   ........................................................................................

3. An interaction between which two spheres was represented by you planting the houseplants in the dirt?

   ........................................................................................

   ........................................................................................

4. If you added a live beetle to your model, what sphere would that represent?

   ........................................................................................

   ........................................................................................

5. What other things could you add to your model to represent different spheres on Earth?

   ........................................................................................

   ........................................................................................

   ........................................................................................

# WEEK 14

# Earth & Space Science
## Water On Earth

5-ESS2-2

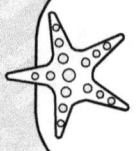

Make observations and gather information about the differences in distribution of water around Earth.

**Directions:** Read the text below. Then answer the questions that follow.

## The Importance Of Water

**Water** is arguably one of the most important resources on Earth. Water is necessary so that plants can make energy and grow. It is used by all living organisms as part of their diets. Water is a habitat where many organisms live, especially aquatic organisms in rivers, lakes and oceans. Water also helps to keep Earth's temperatures more comfortable because it can help move heat away from very hot areas. In this way, water is responsible for weather patterns and climates around the planet.

If you look at a map, you notice that water is found in some areas more than others. A desert has almost no bodies of water whereas an island is completely surrounded by water. Today we will look at where water is found on Earth and how that can impact how humans live.

1. What do plants use water for?

   A. Shelter
   B. To make energy
   C. To make carbon dioxide
   D. Weather

2. Water is responsible for ............................................................ patterns and climate.

   A. Plant
   B. Animal
   C. Aquatic
   D. Weather

3. True or False: deserts and islands are places where you can find similar amounts of water.

   A. True
   B. False

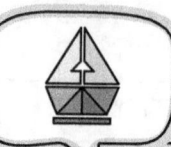
*Yesterday, you learned about the importance of water on Earth and that it is found in different amounts depending on where you are. Today you will explore this further.*

**Directions:** Read each text below and complete the activity. Then answer the questions that follow.

## Coastal Areas

Take a look at a map of the United States. Look at states along the East Coast. The East Coast includes states like Maine, Maryland, Virginia, and Florida. Notice what is to the east of each of these states.

1. What type of large body of water do all of these states border?

    A. The Pacific Ocean

    B. The Gulf of Mexico

    C. The Atlantic Ocean

    D. The Mississippi River

2. Do oceans contain saltwater or freshwater? You can use the Internet to look this up if you are not sure.

    A. Saltwater

    B. Freshwater

## New Mexico Vs. Wisconsin

Using the same map of the United States you used in the last activity, look at the states of New Mexico and Wisconsin. New Mexico's climate is mostly desert whereas Wisconsin has a **temperate** climate which means it has cooler temperatures and plenty of rain for most of the year.

3. Do you see the big lakes on the map next to Wisconsin?

4. Do you see any large lakes near New Mexico?

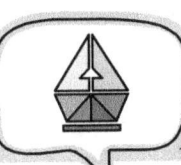
## Where Do You Live?

Think about water that is near your home. Think about if there are streams, rivers, ponds, lakes, oceans, or other bodies of water near you. You may live far away from water or there might be water very close to your home.

**5.** What bodies of water are near your home?

......................................................................................................................................

......................................................................................................................................

......................................................................................................................................

**6.** Do they contain freshwater or saltwater? Ask a parent if you are unsure.

......................................................................................................................................

......................................................................................................................................

......................................................................................................................................

*Yesterday, you explored the different kinds of bodies of water found in different parts of the United States. Today you will explain how this relates to climate and other aspects of those areas.*

**Directions:** Read each text below. Then answer the questions that follow.

## Coastal Areas

You discovered that states on the East Coast all border the Atlantic Ocean, a huge body of saltwater.

**1.** How might the ocean impact the temperature of these states? Refer back to the reading from Day 1 of this week to remind yourself how water can impact the environment.

.......................................................................................................

.......................................................................................................

.......................................................................................................

## New Mexico Vs. Wisconsin

You discovered New Mexico is mostly desert with almost no lakes whereas Wisconsin is near very large lakes and gets a lot of rain.

**2.** Do you think it is more likely to find water in a desert or in an area that has a lot of rain?

.......................................................................................................

.......................................................................................................

**3.** Do you think the lakes near Wisconsin contain freshwater or saltwater?

.......................................................................................................

.......................................................................................................

.......................................................................................................

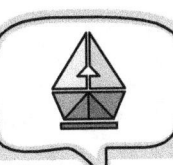

### Where Do You Live?

You discovered that there may be different types of bodies of water near your home and that they could contain either freshwater or saltwater.

**4.** What type of climate do you live in? What type of weather do you often have near your home?

..................................................................................................

..................................................................................................

..................................................................................................

..................................................................................................

..................................................................................................

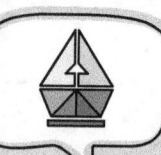
*Yesterday, you explored how different kinds of water can impact the environment they are in. Today you will compare data from different parts of the world and see how the availability of water can impact human life.*

**Background Information:**

Below is a data table that shows data from three different locations on Earth. The data includes how much rainfall the place gets in a year. It also tells you whether or not the location is on a coast and whether or not there are bodies of freshwater in the area. Lastly, the data table shows you what percent of the area can be used to farm food. (The bigger the percent, the more land can be used for farming.)

**Data Table:**

| Place | Average Yearly Rainfall | Is It Coastal? | Does It Have Freshwater Bodies Of Water? | Percent Farmland |
|---|---|---|---|---|
| **Dubai, United Arab Emirates** | 0.4 inches | Yes - Dubai borders the Persian Gulf | No | Less than 1% |
| **Cuba** | 52 inches | Yes - Cuba is an island in the Atlantic Ocean | Yes, including rivers, lakes, and underground springs | 60% |
| **Kampala, Uganda** | 40 inches | No | Yes, from Lake Albert, Lake Victoria, & Lake Kyoga | 35% |

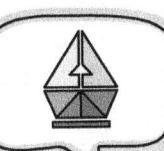

**Follow-up Questions:**

1. What place receives less than an inch of rainfall every year?

2. What place is an island in the Atlantic Ocean?

3. What place has the most farmland?

4. What place is near Lake Victoria?

5. Which two places are coastal?

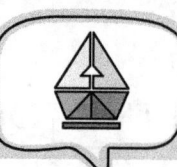
*Yesterday, you analyzed a data table and learned about what types of water can be found in three different places on Earth. Today you will elaborate on this data and draw conclusions about how water availability might impact human life.*

**Directions:** Read and answer each question below.

1. What might be hard about living in Dubai in terms of having access to water?

2. What might be a good thing about living in Cuba in terms of farmland?

3. Why do you think that Cuba gets so much rain every year?

4. People need freshwater in order to live and survive. Which place has the least amount of freshwater?

5. Farmers need freshwater in order to grow plants. Why do you think the United Arab Emirates has very little farmland?

6. Does Uganda have more or less rainfall yearly compared to Cuba?

# WEEK 15

# Earth & Space Science

## Earth's Non-renewable Resources

5-ESS3-1

Read texts and use media to learn about Earth's non-renewable resources and how humans use them.

ARGOPREP

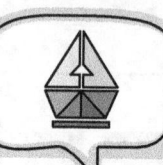
**Directions:** Read the text below. Then answer the questions that follow.

## What Is A Non-Renewable Resource?

You use **resources** every day in your life, many of which are necessary like food, water, and shelter. There are many other things that you use including a computer, television, cars, home appliances, and much more. Many of the materials which power our world are **non-renewable resources**. Non-renewable resources are materials that there is a limited amount of on Earth. This means that if we run out of them, we cannot find or make more of them. Some common non-renewable resources that are used for energy include oil, coal, natural gas, and nuclear energy. Today you will learn about these types of resources and why it is important for us to be conscious about how much we use them.

**1.** Which of these is a resource that is necessary for you?

   **A.** Television

   **B.** Cars

   **C.** A friend

   **D.** Water

**2.** A _____ is a material that there is a limited amount of on Earth.

   **A.** Renewable resource

   **B.** Energy

   **C.** Non-renewable resource

   **D.** Common

**3.** Which of these is NOT a non-renewable resource?

   **A.** Oil

   **B.** Natural gas

   **C.** Coal

   **D.** Solar power

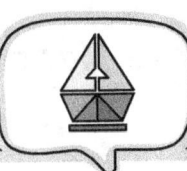
*Yesterday, you learned about non-renewable resources. Today you will explore different kinds of non-renewable resources and how they are used.*

**Directions:** Read each text below and complete the activity. Then answer the question that follows.

## Coal & Oil

Coal and oil are both considered to be **fossil fuels** because they come from the breakdown of fossils over millions and millions of years. Because it takes so long to make coal and oil, we will eventually run out of it. Oil is used to make gasoline, something many people use every day in cars, planes, and home appliances.

1. If your family has a car that runs on gasoline, are you using a non-renewable resource?

   **A.** Yes                                          **B.** No

2. Does flying on a plane use a non-renewable resource?

   **A.** Yes                                          **B.** No

## Natural Gas

Natural gas is obtained by making deep cracks in the Earth's surface and collecting gas in a process called **fracking**. This process can cause pollution which is bad for the environment. Natural gas is used to make electricity and heat for homes and factories. Natural gas can also be used to make products like plastics and fertilizer.

3. Which of the following is natural gas not used for?

   **A.** Heating homes                    **C.** Feeding farm animals

   **B.** Making plastics                    **D.** Powering factories

## Nuclear Power

Some power plants use the powerful energy that comes from nuclear sources. These are types of atoms that give off so much energy that they can create electricity for entire cities or counties. There is a very limited amount of nuclear material on Earth and it needs to be mined in order to collect it. Mining can be bad for the environment.

4. Can nuclear power be used to make electricity?

   **A.** Yes                                          **B.** No

*Yesterday, you learned how different non-renewable resources are used. Today you will explain how using non-renewable resources can impact humans and the environment.*

**Directions:** Read each text below. Then answer the questions that follow.

## Coal & Oil

You discovered that coal and oil take millions of years to make and that they are used to power things like cars and planes.

**1.** If everyone started to use battery-powered cars instead of gas powered cars, what would happen to our supply of coal and oil?

## Natural Gas

You discovered that natural gas is obtained through fracking and that it is used for electricity, heat, and making different products.

**2.** Do you think it is important to recycle products made from non-renewable resources?

**3.** If people stopped using so much plastic, or started recycling more plastic, how might that impact our use of natural gas?

## Nuclear Energy

You discovered that nuclear energy comes from nuclear chemicals which need to be mined. You also learned that they can make a lot of energy for very big areas.

**4.** Why is nuclear power considered to be a non-renewable resource?

.................................................................................................................................

.................................................................................................................................

.................................................................................................................................

.................................................................................................................................

.................................................................................................................................

.................................................................................................................................

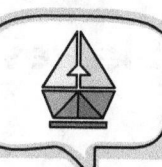
*Yesterday, you explored how using non-renewable resources can impact the Earth and human activity. Today you will analyze data about how different countries use non-renewable resources.*

## Background Information:

Below is a data table that shows data from three different countries. The data includes how much oil the country uses every year. It also includes what percent of the population drive gas-powered cars and the amount of pollution that is created every year.

## Data Table:

| Place | Daily Use Of Oil | Percent of Population That Own Gas Cars | Yearly Amount Of Pollution (greenhouse gases) |
|---|---|---|---|
| United States | 19 million barrels | 85% | 4833 Megatons |
| Russia | 3.5 million barrels | 47% | 1438 Megatons |
| Australia | 1 million barrels | 56% | 392 Megatons |

## Follow-up Questions:

1. What country uses 3.5 millions barrels of oil every day?

.................................................................................................

2. In what country does the biggest percentage of people own gas-powered cars?

.................................................................................................

3. Which country produces the least amount of pollution every year?

.................................................................................................

4. How many barrels of oil does the United States use every day?

.................................................................................................

5. Which country creates 1438 megatons of pollution every year?

.................................................................................................

*Yesterday, you analyzed a data table and learned how three different countries use the non-renewable resource of oil. Today you will elaborate on your findings.*

**Directions:** Read and answer each question below.

**1.** Why is oil a non-renewable resource?

.......................................................................................................................

.......................................................................................................................

.......................................................................................................................

.......................................................................................................................

.......................................................................................................................

**2.** What is one reason the United States uses so much oil?

.......................................................................................................................

.......................................................................................................................

.......................................................................................................................

.......................................................................................................................

.......................................................................................................................

**3.** Why do you think Australia creates the lowest amount of pollution every year?

.......................................................................................................................

.......................................................................................................................

.......................................................................................................................

.......................................................................................................................

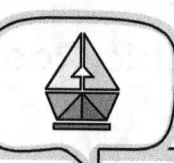
**4.** If Russia wanted to lower the amount of oil it uses every year, what could it do?

**5.** Humans use a lot of oil every single day. Do you think it is important to slow or stop the use of non-renewable resources?

# Earth & Space Science

## Earth's Renewable Resources

5-ESS3-1

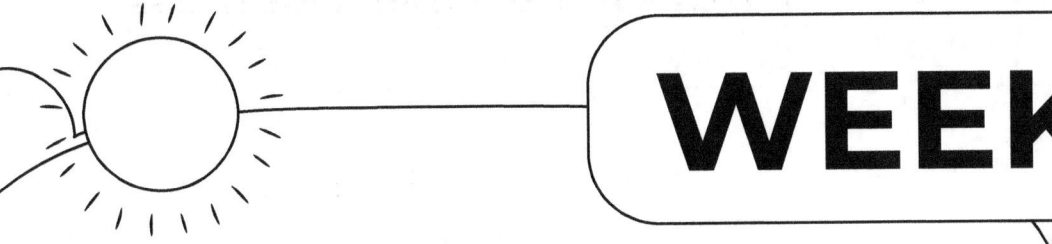

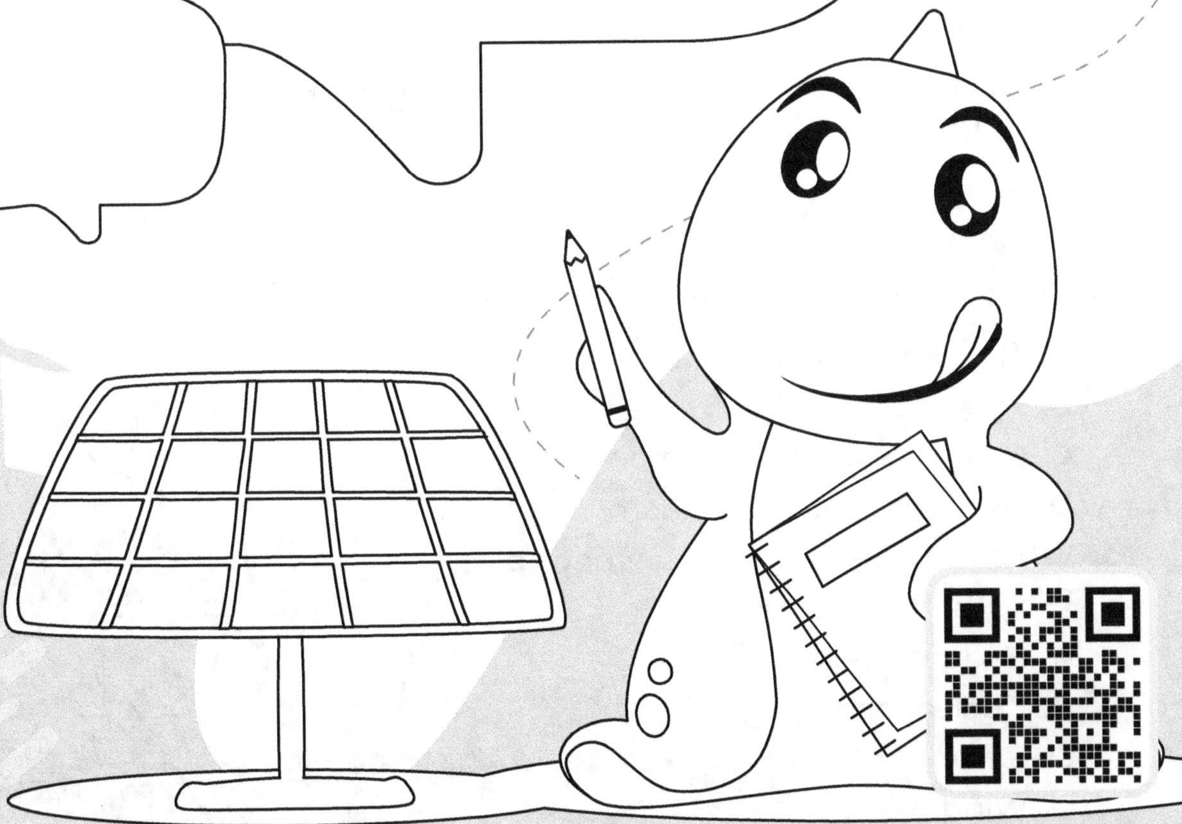

Read texts and use media to learn about Earth's renewable resources and how humans use them.

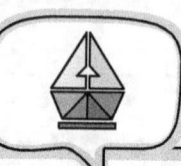
**Directions:** Read the text below. Then answer the questions that follow.

## What Is A Renewable Resource?

Last week you learned about non-renewable resources and the importance of slowing or stopping our use of them. Today we will discuss **renewable resources** and why it is important to use these resources for things like energy and heat. A renewable resource is something that we can make or find more of no matter how much we use it. Many renewable resources have the added benefit of making less pollution than non-renewable resources. Renewable resources that can be used for heat and energy include solar, wind, geothermal, and hydropower energy. Today you will learn how energy can be obtained from these resources and how humans can use them in ways that are generally better for the environment than the use of non-renewable resources

**1.** Can you make or find more of something that is considered to be a renewable resource?

    **A.** Yes

    **B.** No

**2.** What is one benefit of renewable resources?

    **A.** They smell good

    **B.** They include oil and coal

    **C.** Some create less pollution

    **D.** Humans cannot use them

**3.** Which of these is NOT a renewable resource?

    **A.** Hydropower

    **B.** Nuclear energy

    **C.** Solar

    **D.** Wind

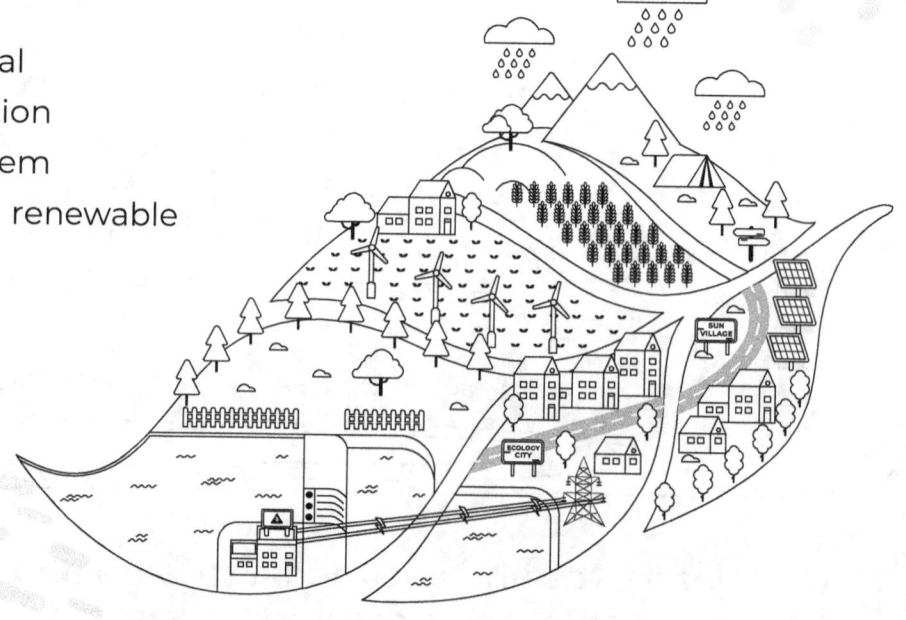

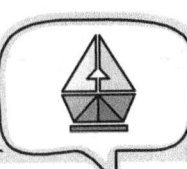
*Yesterday, you learned about renewable resources and the benefits of using them. Today you will explore different kinds of renewable resources and how they are used.*

**Directions:** Read each text below and complete the activity. Then answer the question that follows.

## Wind & Solar Power

The Earth has no shortage of sunlight and wind which means power from these sources is relatively unlimited. Wind energy can be captured with a structure called a **wind turbine** and converted into electricity. Solar power can be captured with **solar panels** and converted into both heat and electricity. Both of these types of renewable energy do little damage to the environment.

**1.** What structure can capture the energy of the wind?

.................................................................................................................

**2.** What structure can capture the energy of the sun?

.................................................................................................................

## Hydropower

Water in rivers is always flowing. Similar to wind power, water can be used to turn **turbines**. The movement of turbines can create electricity which can be used to power entire cities. Dams, a huge structure that controls the flow of water from a lake or river, often have turbines in them to generate power.

**3.** Why is hydropower considered a renewable resource?

.................................................................................................................

.................................................................................................................

## Geothermal

Heat energy can be captured from below the Earth's surface. The inside of Earth is hot and molten (like lava) which means it gives off a ton of heat. This heat from Earth's core can be captured and used to heat homes and can also be converted into electricity. Earth's core will give off heat for millions of years to come making it a renewable resource.

**4.** What is very hot and can be used to make geothermal energy?

A. Wind

B. Earth's surface

C. Water

D. Earth's core

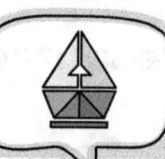
*Yesterday, you learned how different renewable resources are used. Today you will explain how using renewable resources can impact humans and the environment.*

**Directions:** Read each text below. Then answer the questions that follow.

## Wind & Solar Power

You discovered that wind and solar power require structures like wind turbines and solar panels in order to capture energy.

**1.** Where would be a good place to put solar panels?

   **A.** A place that gets a lot of sun

   **B.** A forest with lots of shade

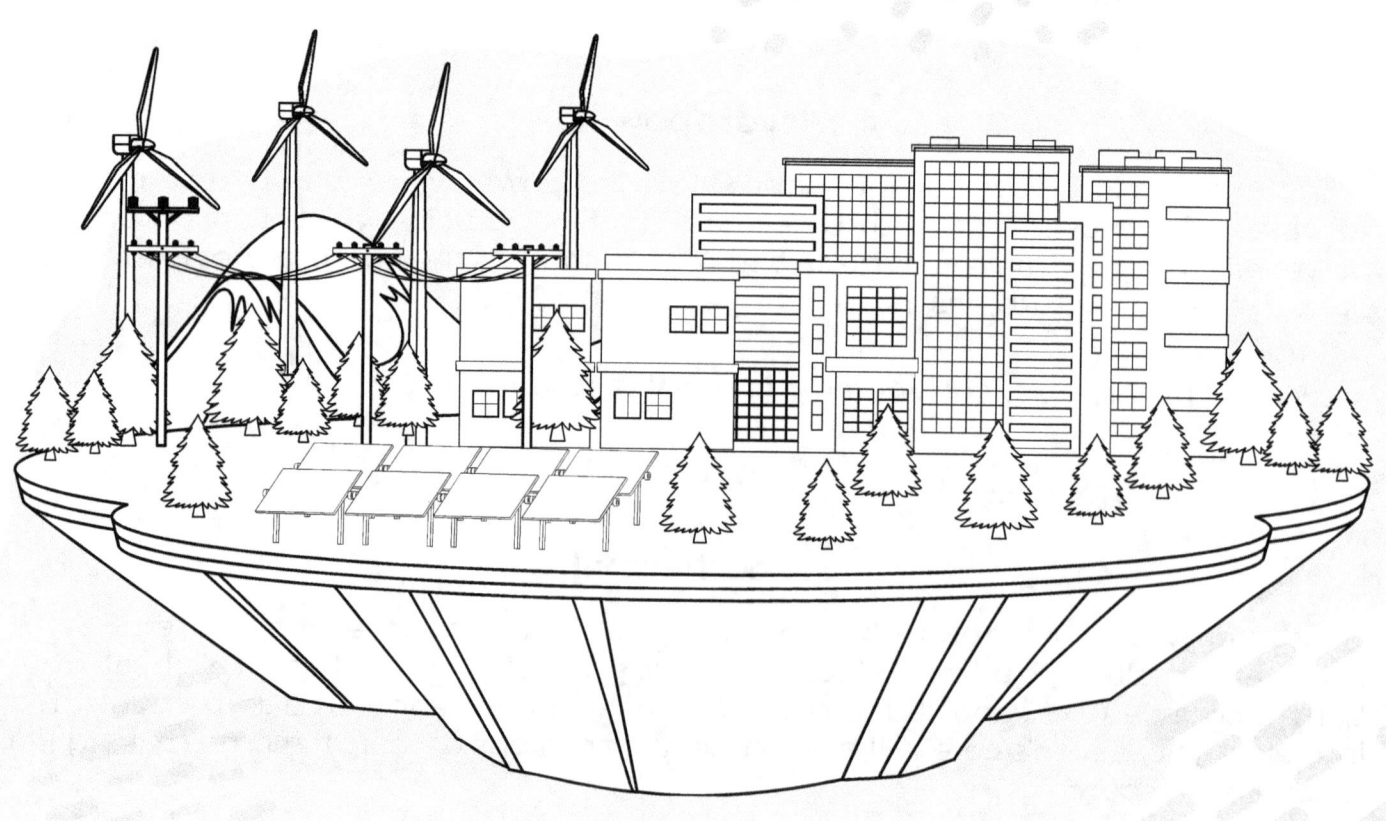

**2.** Where would be a challenging place to put wind turbines? Wind turbines can be dozens of stories tall and often need a lot of space because the blades on them are very wide. Search for a picture of one on the Internet if it would be helpful to look at one for this question.

..................................................................................................................

..................................................................................................................

..................................................................................................................

..................................................................................................................

..................................................................................................................

..................................................................................................................

## Hydropower

You discovered that the movement of water can be turned into energy using turbines.

**3.** If a river always has a constant supply of water, will it always have a constant supply of hydropower?

**A.** Yes

**B.** No

## Geothermal

You discovered that heat from the Earth's core can be captured as geothermal energy.

**4.** What would be a place on the planet that would benefit a lot from geothermal heat?

..................................................................................................................

..................................................................................................................

..................................................................................................................

..................................................................................................................

..................................................................................................................

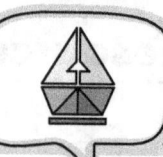
*Yesterday, you explored how renewable resources can be used and where they can be used. Today you will create a model of a hydropower turbine.*

### Materials:

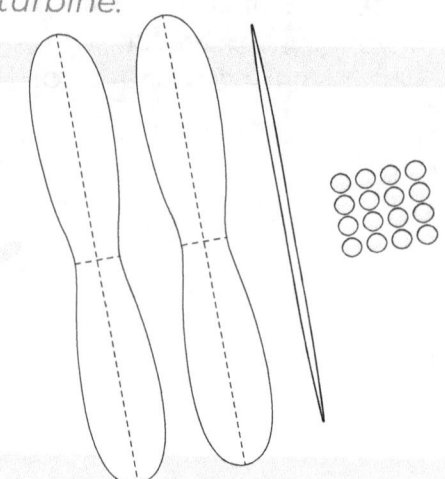

1. A clear plastic box about the size of a shoebox
2. Dirt
3. Water
4. Popsicle sticks
5. Toothpicks
6. Craft glue or a glue gun
7. 2 large plastic beads or pony beads

### Procedure:

1. Take the plastic box and fill it about $\frac{3}{4}$ full with dirt, making sure the dirt slants down towards one end of the box to create a hill. Pack the dirt down so that it is pretty solid in the box.

2. Use your fingers or a spoon to dig out a channel down the middle of the dirt from the top of the hill to the bottom of the hill. This represents a river.

3. Cut two popsicle sticks into 4 equal pieces - this means you should have 8 total small pieces of popsicle sticks. Glue the pieces together around a toothpick so that they make a star (✳) pattern. It should look like the spokes on a bicycle wheel and the toothpick should stick through the middle so that there is some popsicle stick on either side of the center of the star.

4. Place two pony beads on either end of the popsicle stick and place it centers in the river at the top of the dirt hill in your box. The turbine that you have now made out of popsicle sticks should not touch the bottom of the river but be held just floating in it thanks to the pony beads.

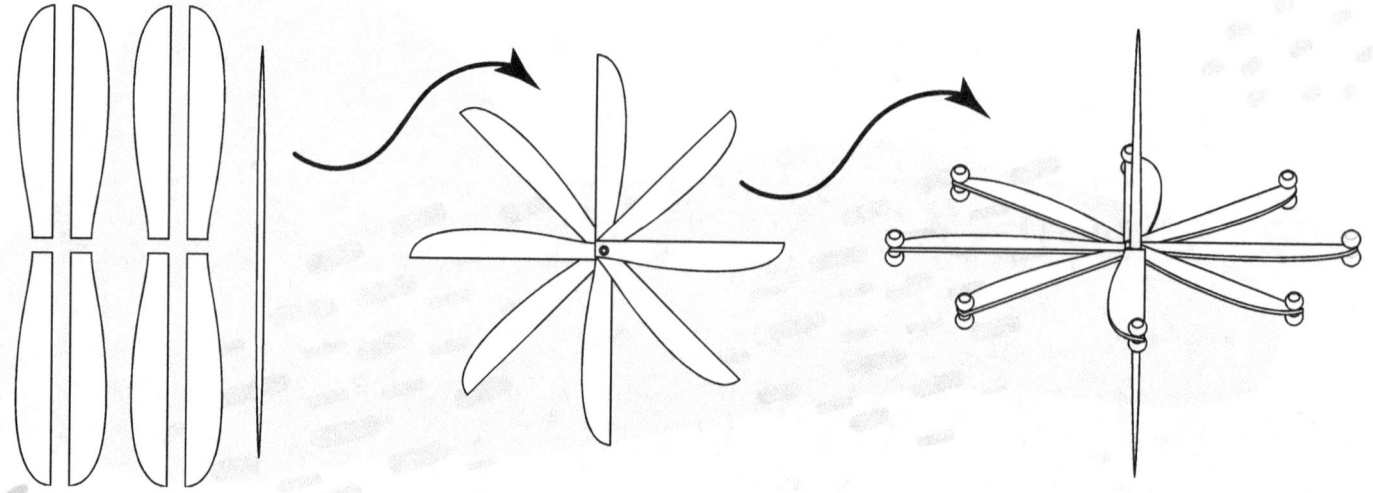

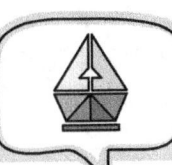
5. Take a cup of water and pour it right behind the turbine into the beginning of the river at the top of the hill in your box. Notice how the popsicle stick turbine moves as you pour water into the river behind it.

**Follow-up Questions:**

1. What did the river have flowing through it?

..................................................................................................................................

2. What happens to the turbine when you pour water into the river?

..................................................................................................................................

3. What type of power are turbines associated with that involves water?

..................................................................................................................................

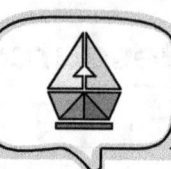
*Yesterday, you created a model of a hydropower turbine. Today you will elaborate on how your model worked.*

**Directions:** Read and answer each question below.

**1.** When a hydropower turbine moves, what does it create?

_____

_____

**2.** Would this be a good renewable resource to have in the desert? Why or why not?

_____

_____

**3.** What is one benefit of hydropower energy over the non-renewable resource coal?

_____

_____

_____

**4.** What is one thing you could improve about the model you made?

_____

_____

_____

_____

_____

**5.** Can you think of another way to make a model of a different kind of renewable resource such as solar or wind?

....................................................................................................................

....................................................................................................................

....................................................................................................................

....................................................................................................................

....................................................................................................................

....................................................................................................................

....................................................................................................................

....................................................................................................................

# WEEK 17

# Engineering
## Design Problems

3-5-ETS1-1

Develop a model or an illustration that proposes a solution to the product or problem, clearly defining how its form relates to its function.

ARGOPREP

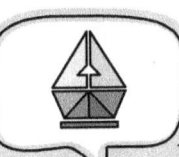
**Directions:** Read the text below. Then answer the questions that follow.

## Designing The Perfect Plan

When you look around you, you may notice that items in your house aren't perfect in some way. For example, maybe there is a countertop that is too tall for shorter people in your home. Or maybe the mouth of a glass is so wide that when you take a drink from it, you often spill some of your drink on yourself. There is nothing wrong with something being imperfect, but if you notice something could be improved, why not try to make it better? In science and engineering, these are known as **design problems.** People can spend their entire lives working to solve these problems so that products and processes are even better. Today we will focus on how to identify problems or imperfections so that you can eventually design a plan to fix them.

1. If a kitchen countertop is really tall, what type of person might that be a problem for?

   **A.** Tall people

   **B.** People who don't cook

   **C.** Short people

   **D.** It isn't a problem for anyone

2. True or False: When you notice a problem or an imperfection, you can create a plan to solve the problem and make it better.

   **A.** True

   **B.** False

3. In science and engineering, what is an issue or an imperfection with a product or process called?

   **A.** A design problem

   **B.** A solution

   **C.** An improvement

   **D.** A plan

*Yesterday, you learned about design problems and that identifying them can help lead to a way to fix them. Today you will try to identify design problems in a few examples.*

**Directions:** Read each text below and analyze what the design problem might be. Then answer the questions that follow.

## Do You See What I See?

Elenor has a really cool 3-D picture book that she decides to bring over to her friend Chad's house one day. She shows him how when you put on the 3-D glasses, it takes the red and blue images and makes them pop out at you. When Chad puts the glasses on, he cannot see the images in 3-D. He explains to Elenor that he is partially colorblind and has a hard time seeing the color red.

**1.** For Chad, what is a design issue with the 3-D picture book and why?

_____

_____

_____

## Left Vs. Right

Damien and Rocky are working on a project where they need to cut out paper squares for a board game they've created. Damien is right-handed and has no problem cutting out neat paper squares. Rocky is left-handed and the sciessor are very awkward to hold, making it very hard for him to cut out paper squares.

**2.** How are Damien and Rocky different?

_____

_____

**3.** What is the design problem with the scissor?

_____

_____

### Birds Of A Feather

Ananya has designed a birdhouse that has a clear plastic wall on one side so she can look into it and see what birds are nesting in it. She is hoping that a cardinal will make a home in the birdhouse. Cardinals are larger birds that can be up to 9 inches tall. When Ananya visits the birdhouse she only notices painted buntings visiting it. Painted buntings are smaller, about 5 inches tall.

**4.** What is one explanation for why cardinals might not be making a nest in Ananya's birdhouse?

......................................................................................................................

......................................................................................................................

......................................................................................................................

......................................................................................................................

......................................................................................................................

......................................................................................................................

*Yesterday, you identified different problems with the design of different items. Today you will explain in more detail what the problems are and how they might be solved.*

**Directions:** Read each text below. Then answer the questions that follow.

## Do You See What I See?

You discovered that a red and blue 3-D picture book does not look the same for a person who is partially colorblind.

**1.** What might be a solution to this problem?

_____

_____

_____

## Left Vs. Right

You discovered that scissors designed for right-handed people do not work very well for left-handed people.

**2.** What might be a solution to this problem?

_____

_____

**3.** Is it important to design products for all types of people?

    **A.** Yes

    **B.** No

## Birds Of A Feather

You discovered that Ananya's birdhouse worked well for painted buntings but not for cardinals, most likely because it was too small for cardinals to nest in it.

**4.** If Ananya wanted to make a new birdhouse, what could she do to make sure cardinals were able to nest in it?

_____

_____

_____

*Yesterday, you explained how to improve different design problems that you identified. Today you will experiment with designing the best possible paper airplane.*

## Materials:

1. A computer
2. A notebook
3. 15-20 sheets of white paper copy paper (make sure to recycle when you are done)
4. A ruler
5. A meter stick
6. A pencil
7. A large, open space (like your backyard or an open field in a park)

## Procedure:

1. Start by researching paper airplanes on the Internet. Look for instructional websites or videos that show you how to make and fold different designs for paper airplanes. Pick at least 4 different designs that are somewhat simple to make.
2. Make one of each of your 4 different designs. It's okay to try them a few times! Practice makes perfect. You might need a ruler to make sure your measurements are correct for some designs.
3. Go into an open field and mark a starting spot with a rock or a stick. Throw each of your planes one at a time and then measure how far each one went. Throw and measure each plane's distance 5 times and record your findings in the table below.
4. Circle the furthest distance each plane flew once you've collected your data.

## Data Table:

|  | Plane #1 | Plane #2 | Plane #3 | Plane #4 |
|---|---|---|---|---|
| **Distance of 1st Throw** |  |  |  |  |
| **Distance of 2nd Throw** |  |  |  |  |
| **Distance of 3rd Throw** |  |  |  |  |
| **Distance of 4th Throw** |  |  |  |  |
| **Distance of 5th Throw** |  |  |  |  |

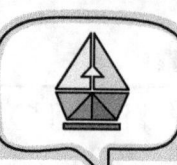
*Yesterday, you created 4 different paper planes and measured how far they flew. Today you will elaborate on your data and try to determine if there were any design problems in any of the planes you made.*

**Directions:** Read and answer each question below.

1. Which plane flew the furthest distance?

2. Which plane flew the shortest distance?

3. What is one thing about the design of the plane that flew the furthest that might make it a particularly good design?

4. What is one thing about the design of the plane that flew the shortest distance that you might want to improve or change?

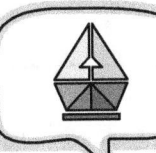
**5.** What is one thing you could do to all of the planes in order to make them fly farther? Be creative! Let your imagination run wild.

........................................................................................

........................................................................................

........................................................................................

........................................................................................

........................................................................................

........................................................................................

........................................................................................

........................................................................................

........................................................................................

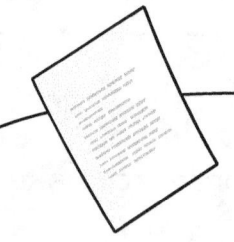

# WEEK 18

# Engineering
## Comparing Solutions

3-5-ETS1-2

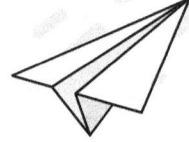

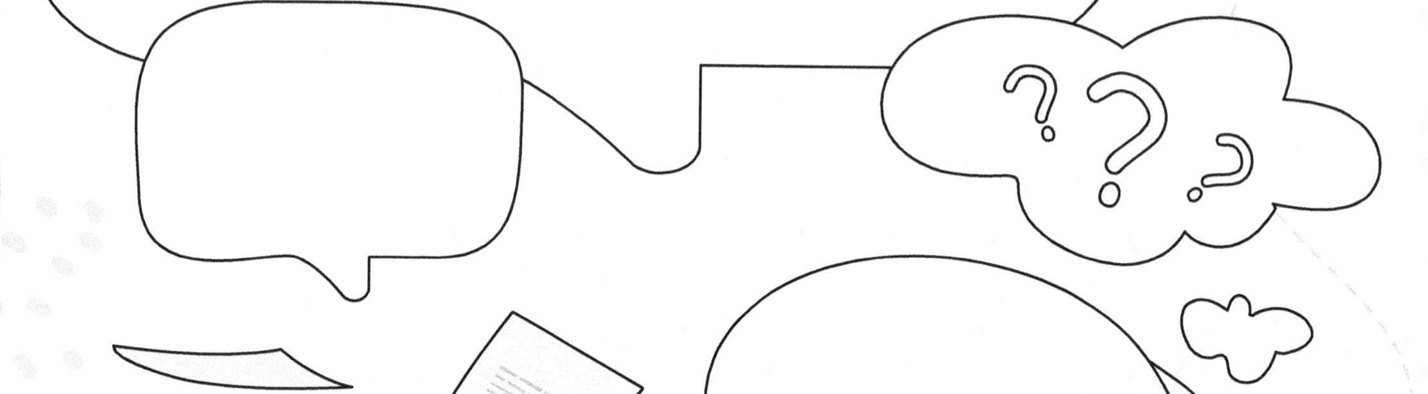

Analyze the data from testing and compare the effectiveness of different solutions.

ARGOPREP

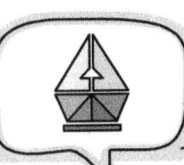
**Directions:** Read the text below. Then answer the questions that follow.

## What Is The Best Solution?

Last week you practiced identifying design problems and creating solutions to improve them. Today you will explore how to compare solutions. If you think about it, there could be a huge number of solutions to the same problems. For example, if you had a recipe for a cake that resulted in a cake that did not taste good, you could try to change a lot of things about the recipe. Maybe you would add more or less of an ingredient like flour or sugar. Maybe you would change how long you bake it for. Maybe you would add an extra ingredient like chocolate or vanilla.

When it comes to fixing a design problem, you want to try out multiple solutions in order to determine which one is the best solution to your problem. A good solution fixes the problem and does not create new design problems.

1. A way to fix any design problem is to compare ............................................................

    A. Solutions

    B. Problems

    C. Recipes

    D. Ingredients

2. True or False: A good solution should create new design problems.

    A. True

    B. False

3. If you only tested one solution, you wouldn't be able to do what?

    A. Fix a design problem

    B. Compare different solutions

    C. Make a cake

    D. Create a new design problem

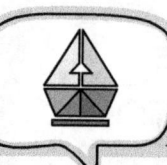
*Yesterday, you learned about the importance of comparing different solutions to the same design problem. Today you will explore this process by analyzing possible solutions to various design problems.*

**Directions:** Read each text below and analyze what the design problem might be. Then answer the question that follows.

### A Very Tipsy Cup

Let's pretend you have a lidless cup that always seems to get spilled. It is very easy to knock over because it has a very narrow base. Also, when you take a drink from it, the mouth of the cup is so wide that liquid gets all over your face.

1. Draw what you think the cup looks like in the box below.

**2.** Which of the following are possible solutions to the problem? Choose any that apply.

A. Make the mouth of the cup wider

B. Make the base of the cup wider

C. Make a lid for the cup

D. Make the cup tall and thin

## Fast Food

Shelly has some friends coming over to visit and wants to make a pizza. Unfortunately, the recipe she found for pizza takes an hour and they are going to be there in only 30 minutes. Shelly does not have any money to buy any additional ingredients or food.

**3.** Do you see how time is going to limit the solutions Shelly can consider?

A. Yes

B. No

**4.** Can Shelly use the solution of ordering delivery pizza for her friends instead?

A. Yes

B. No

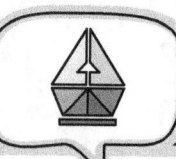
## Energy & The Environment

Timi wants to reduce the amount of electricity he uses every day because he knows this is good for the environment.

**5.** What are some solutions to help Timi reduce his use of electricity?

.............................................................................................................

.............................................................................................................

.............................................................................................................

.............................................................................................................

.............................................................................................................

.............................................................................................................

*Yesterday, you identified different solutions to a design problem. Today you will explain how you might compare solutions and pick the best one for each design problem.*

**Directions:** Read each text below. Then answer the questions that follow.

## A Very Tipsy Cup

You discovered that a cup which spills often could be improved by adding a lid or making the base of it wider so that it does not tip over as easily.

1. What solution would be more useful to you if you were worried about spilling on yourself when taking a sip of a drink?

## Fast Food

You discovered Shelly's problem of making pizza for her friends was constrained (made harder) by having only a little bit of time and no money to order delivery.

2. What could Shelly do in order to provide food for her guests in only 30 minutes?

3. When you don't have unlimited resources, such as money or time, do you have more or less possible solutions to compare?

   A. More

   B. Less

## Energy & The Environment

You discovered that Timi can reduce his use of electricity in lots of different ways if he wants to be more environmentally conscious.

4. Which of the following solutions would reduce Timi's electricity use and allow Timi to live normally?

   A. Timi never charges his cell phone.

   B. Timi turns off lights when he leaves the room.

   C. Timi gets rid of all of his appliances and just burns candles for light.

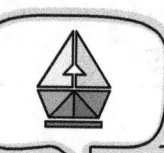
*Yesterday, you explained how some solutions to design problems might be better than others. You also saw that sometimes there can be constraints on what solutions are possible. Today you will explore different solutions to a particular design problem.*

## Background Information:

A group of students have designed a dog bed that they claim is more comfortable than any other dog bed on the market. They give the dog bed to 5 of their friends who have dogs and ask them to give them some feedback on their design. Below is a data table which shows how the dogs responded to the new bed versus their old bed.

## Data Table:

| | How many hours a day did it sleep on the old bed? | How many hours a day did it sleep on the new bed? | Did the dog fit in the bed comfortably? | Other observations? |
|---|---|---|---|---|
| **Dog #1** | 4 | 5 | No | None |
| **Dog #2** | 6 | 6 | Yes | The dog sniffed the new bed a lot. |
| **Dog #3** | 1 | 10 | Yes | The bed was the perfect size for my chihuahua! |
| **Dog #4** | 5 | 4 | No | The dog did not seem to like the smell of the new bed. I washed it and he spent more time sleeping on it. |
| **Dog #5** | 4 | 6 | No | I thought the new bed sort of smelled like plastic. |

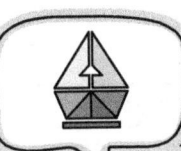
**Follow-Up Questions:**

**1.** Which dog seemed to like the new bed best?

......................................................................................................

**2.** What was the most common observation in terms of how the dog fit in the bed?

......................................................................................................

**3.** Does there seem to be an overall preference for the new dog bed versus the dog's old dog bed?

    **A.** Yes

    **B.** No

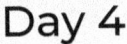

*Yesterday, you analyzed data from observations made on a design for a new dog bed. The new dog bed did not seem any more comfortable to the dogs than their old bed overall. Today you will elaborate on those findings and help determine what design problems might need a solution.*

Directions: Read and answer each question below.

1. Do you think the new dog bed design has any design problems based on the feedback?

    **A.** Yes

    **B.** No

2. In order to make this dog bed more comfortable for dogs of different sizes, what could the designers do?

    ................................................................................

    ................................................................................

3. Many people said either they or their dogs noticed a smell on the new bed that was unpleasant. What is a possible solution to this design problem?

    ................................................................................

    ................................................................................

4. What could be another challenge of designing a dog bed?

    ................................................................................

    ................................................................................

5. If you could redesign something that you use every day, what would you choose to make a new version of?

    ................................................................................

    ................................................................................

    ................................................................................

# Engineering
## Design On A Dime

3-5-ETS1-1

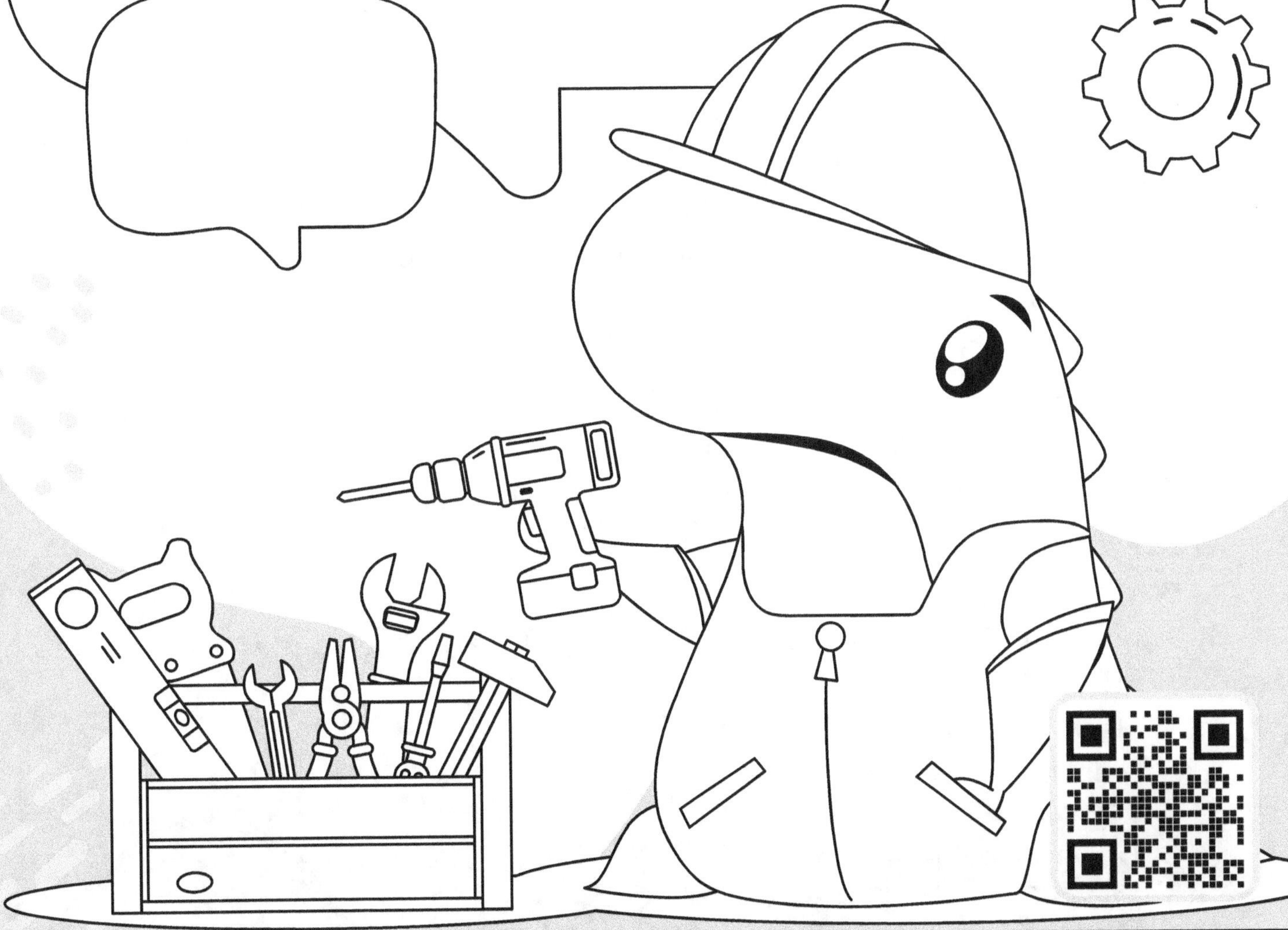

Develop a step-by-step process to test your model/idea when resources are limited.

ARGOPREP

**Directions:** Read the text below. Then answer the questions that follow.

## Creating A Solution On A Budget

Last week, you explored the importance of comparing different solutions to a problem. You saw that there could be many possible options for solutions. Sometimes, however, you might be **constrained** by different things such as time or money. Constraints mean that only some solutions will be possible. Constraints limit what solutions will work for a given design problem.

For example, if you need to complete a project in an hour, you should not choose a solution that will take two hours. It would not be a good solution. Similarly, when scientists and engineers are designing solutions to design problems, they might need to stay within a budget or stick to specific requests made by the people they are designing for.

**1.** What might make it so that only some solutions are possible?

    **A.** Unlimited money

    **B.** Constraints

    **C.** Design problems

    **D.** Unlimited time

**2.** If I have only $10 to spend on a project, is a solution that costs $20 a good option?

    **A.** Yes

    **B.** No

**3.** If you want to design a roller coaster made of steel, which one of these might be a constraint on your design?

    **A.** How long you have to build it

    **B.** The cost of steel

    **C.** How much space it can take up in the theme park

    **D.** All of these could be constraints

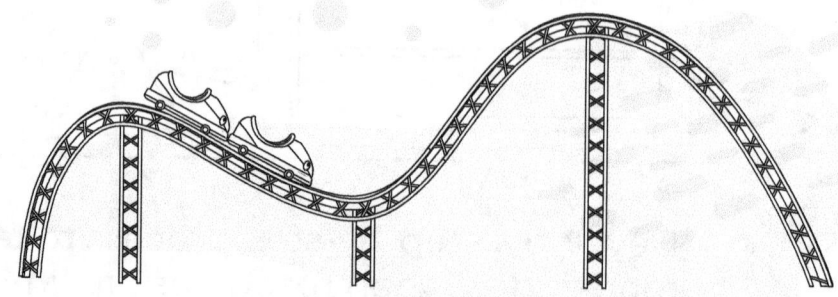

*Yesterday, you learned that sometimes there can be constraints that limit what solutions are possible when trying to fix a design problem. Today you will explore this idea further.*

**Directions:** Read each text below and analyze what the constraints might be. Then answer the question that follows.

### The Perfect Milk Container

Milk is something a lot of people have in their refrigerator. If your family drinks milk, you might have to buy it every week. A gallon of milk often comes in a plastic or a glass container which can either be recycled or reused. A gallon container needs to be strong enough to hold the milk but light enough for you to pour the milk into a glass.

**1.** If you sold milk, would you want the gallon milk container to be expensive or inexpensive?

   **A.** Expensive

   **B.** Inexpensive

### Designing A Rocket

Engineers who build rockets need their designs to fit a lot of constraints. It needs to be strong enough to travel into space but it also needs to be light enough so that fuel can propel it into space.

**2.** What are two things that engineers must consider when designing a rocket?

...........................................................................................................

...........................................................................................................

### Recycled & Reused

Jote loves to sew and wants to start making reusable shopping bags out of old clothes and sheets that people do not use any more. This is a great idea for a couple different reasons. First off, she is recycling things that might otherwise be thrown away. Second, she encourages people to use reusable shopping bags. Lastly, the recycled clothing and sheets are much cheaper to purchase at a thrift store than if she were to buy brand new fabric at a craft store.

**3.** Do you see how Jote is able to save money by using recycled items for her bags?

   **A.** Yes

   **B.** No

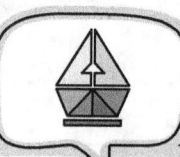
*Yesterday, you identified some constraints to different design problems. Today you will explain how those constraints might affect possible solutions.*

**Directions:** Read each text below. Then answer the questions that follow.

## The Perfect Milk Container

You discovered that a gallon milk container should be strong but also cheap to make since people often recycle it after the milk is gone.

**1.** Why would you not want to choose to make a gallon milk container out of platinum, a heavy and expensive metal?

_____

_____

_____

_____

## Designing A Rocket

You discovered that engineers must balance making a rocket that is strong enough to travel into space but also light enough so it can lift off of the ground.

**2.** What is one material that probably would not be good to use when designing a rocket?

    **A.** Shatter-proof glass

    **B.** Lighter metals

    **C.** Paper

    **D.** Heat-resistant plastic

## Recycled & Reused

You discovered that using recycled materials when designing something is not only good for the environment, but it can be cheaper as well.

**3.** Which constraint could using recycled materials related to?

    **A.** Time

    **B.** Weight

    **C.** Diet

    **D.** Budget

*Yesterday, you explained how some solutions to design problems might be better than others depending on what constraints there might be. Today you will try designing a solution with constraints in mind.*

**Materials:**

1. Recyclables (such as cereal boxes, plastic food containers, old newspapers, etc.)
   - Make sure to choose things that are relatively clean and easy to work with.
2. Scissors
3. Ruler
4. Glue and/or tape
5. Bird seed

**Procedure & Questions:**

Today you will design a bird feeder that you can hang outside your home. It should be able to hold bird seed and be made entirely out of recyclable materials. Go through the following steps and answer the questions as you go.

1. What are you designing today?

   ....................................................................................................................

2. Look at the recyclables you have and list out below what each one is made of. For example, a cereal box is made out of cardboard.

   ....................................................................................................................

   ....................................................................................................................

   ....................................................................................................................

3. What types of qualities should your bird feeder have? Should it be light or heavy? Should it be strong or flimsy? What makes a good bird feeder?

   ....................................................................................................................

   ....................................................................................................................

   ....................................................................................................................

   ....................................................................................................................

   ....................................................................................................................

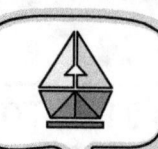
**4.** Below, draw two possible designs of what you want your bird feeder to look like. You can always go on the computer and research what different bird feeders look like for inspiration.

| Design #1 | Design #2 |
|-----------|-----------|
|           |           |

**5.** Pick a design and build it with your materials. Hang it outside with bird seed in it and observe if birds use it or if you see any design problems. It might be a few days before you notice birds using it. Birds need time to learn where your awesome bird feeder is.

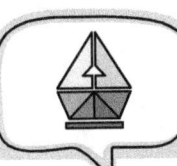
*Yesterday, you designed a bird feeder using recycled materials. Today you will elaborate on any constraints that you noticed and how you designed solutions for them.*

**Directions:** Read and answer each question below.

1. Do you want a bird feeder to be light or heavy? Hint: it needs to hang on a tree or a bush.

   A. Light

   B. Heavy

2. Do you want a bird feeder to be strong or flimsy? Hint: It needs to hold both seed and the weight of a bird.

   A. Strong

   B. Flimsy

3. Which recyclable material is best with these two constraints in mind?

   A. Cardboard

   B. Recycled newspaper

   C. Plastic

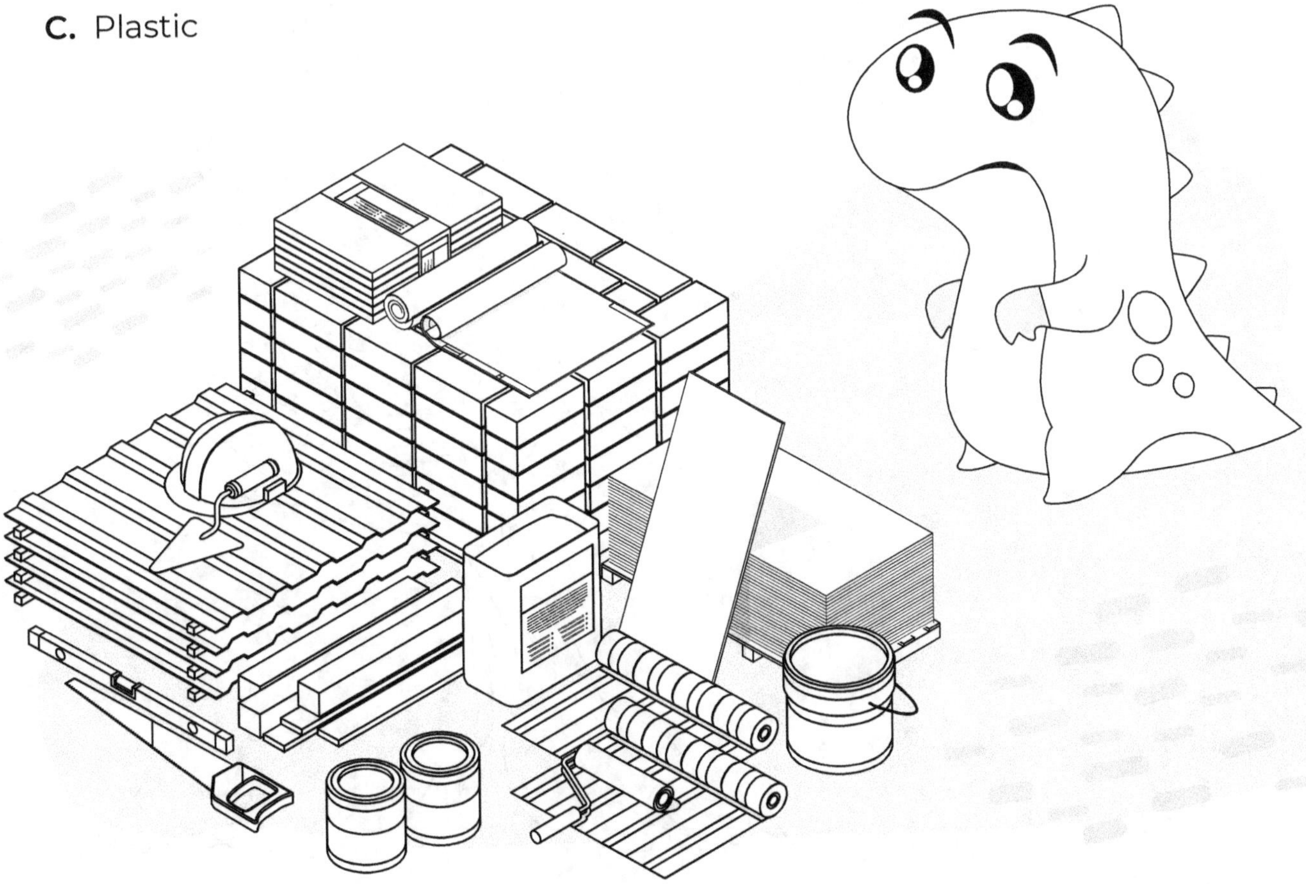

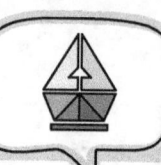
**4.** What did you like best about your design?

........................................................................................

........................................................................................

........................................................................................

........................................................................................

........................................................................................

........................................................................................

........................................................................................

**5.** What could be improved with your design?

........................................................................................

........................................................................................

........................................................................................

........................................................................................

........................................................................................

........................................................................................

........................................................................................

........................................................................................

........................................................................................

# Engineering
## Improving Models

3-5-ETS1-3

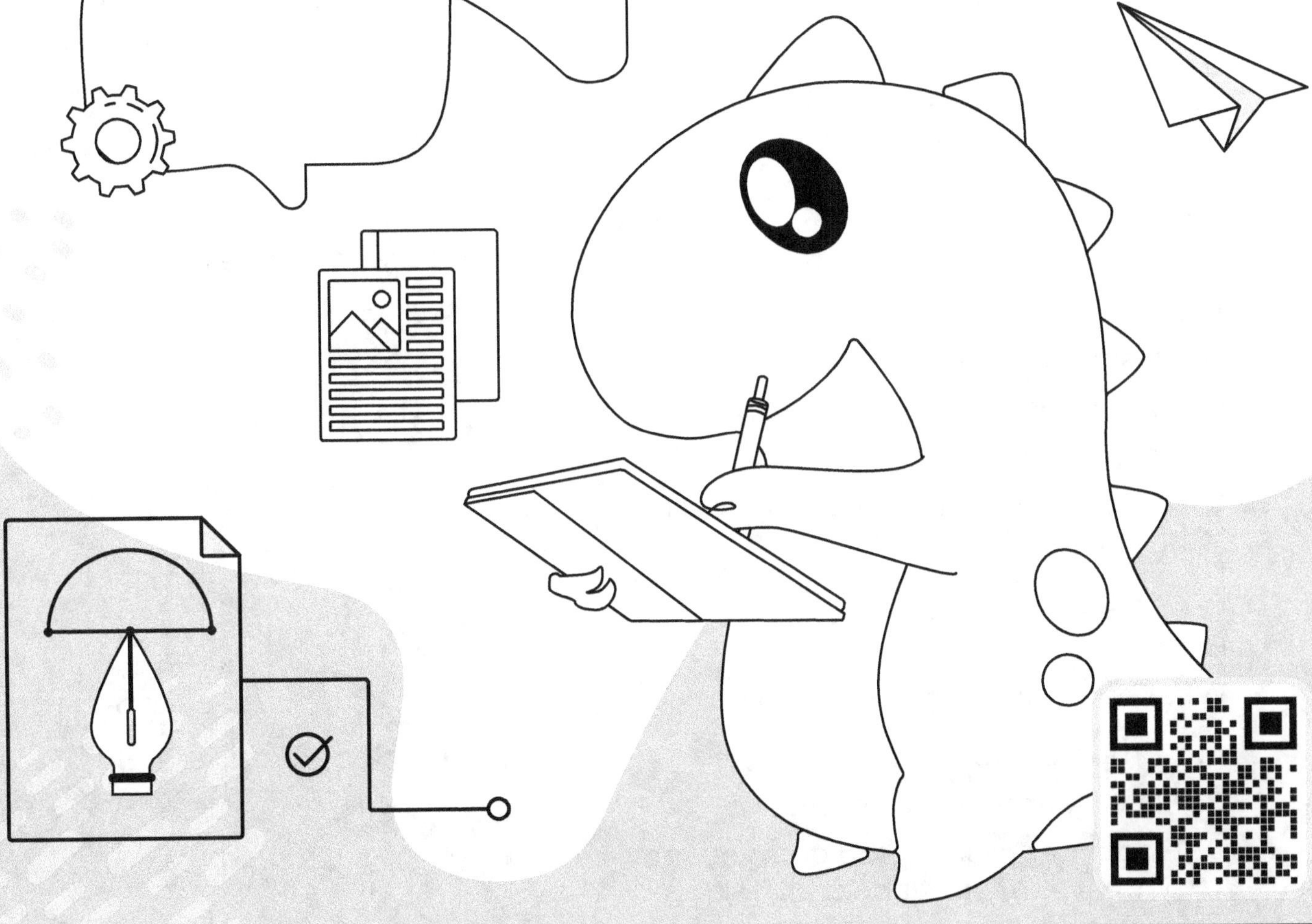

Re-design an original idea and expand on the idea that editing ideas is an important part of the process.

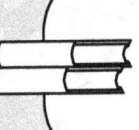

ARGOPREP

**Directions:** Read the text below. Then answer the questions that follow.

## Improving Your Ideas With Prototypes

When trying to design a product or an idea, it is important to start with a plan first as you have learned over the past few weeks. It is also important to identify problems and solutions which may arise. One way to help with planning a design and making it better is to create what is called a **prototype**. A prototype is sort of like a first draft of an idea or a design. It helps you decide what parts of your idea are good and what parts need to be changed so that there are no design problems in your final design. For example, if a scientist were designing a new plastic bottle which used 25% less plastic than other models, they would probably make a few prototypes and compare them. They might consider which one holds the most water. Or they might consider which one feels better to hold. Prototypes can help you take an idea and compare solutions more easily.

1. _____ are like first drafts of a design or an idea.

   A. Solutions

   B. Design problems

   C. Water bottles

   D. Prototypes

2. Can you change things with your design after making a prototype?

   A. Yes

   B. No

3. What can a prototype help you do?

   A. Compare solutions

   B. Make your final idea better

   C. Find other design problems you may not have thought about at first

   D. All of the above

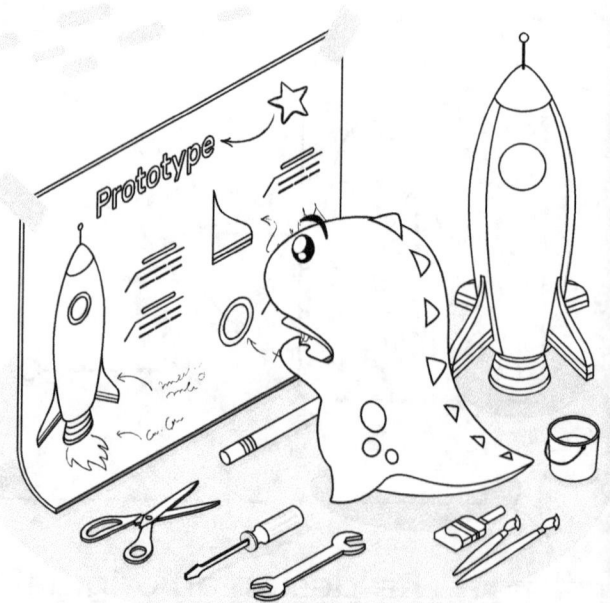

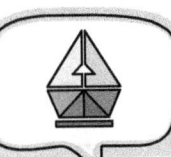
*Yesterday, you learned that prototypes can help you make your final design or solution to a problem even better. Today you will identify problems with prototypes.*

**Directions:** Read each text below and analyze what the constraints might be. Then answer the question that follows.

### A Better Chair

Find a chair in your home and observe it. Notice what it looks like, how it feels when you sit in it, what it is made of, or anything else you notice.

**1.** What is one thing that you could improve about this chair and why?

......................................................................................................................

......................................................................................................................

### More Candy Please!

Pretend you are designing a bag for a company which makes a new kind of candy. You make a prototype of the bag and fill it with as much candy as it will hold. You find that it holds 20 pieces of candy but the company wants it to hold at least 25 pieces of candy.

**2.** What will you need to change in order to make your final design of the candy bag better?

......................................................................................................................

......................................................................................................................

**3.** Was it good that you made a prototype to test out your design?

    **A.** Yes                                  **B.** No

### Perfect Cube

Take a piece of clay and try to mold it into a perfect cube, like the shape of a dice. Measure each side and see if they are the same. If the sides are not all the same, try re-molding the clay so that it is more like a cube. Try to get your clay into as perfect a cube as you can.

**4.** Do you see how your first attempt was like a prototype of your final cube?

    **A.** Yes                                  **B.** No

*Yesterday, you identified some design problems in prototypes that you made or thought about. Today you will talk about what changes you would make to a final design based on these observations.*

**Directions:** Read each text below. Then answer the questions that follow.

## A Better Chair

You discovered that a chair in your home can be improved in some way.

1.  Look back at what you want to improve with the chair. Draw what the new chair could look like below.

### More Candy Please!

You discovered that by making a prototype of a candy bag, you learned that you needed to make your final design bigger.

**2.** If the company wanted you to make another bag that fit 10 pieces of candy, what would you have to do to your design?

.................................................................................................................

.................................................................................................................

.................................................................................................................

### Perfect Cube

You discovered that molding a perfect cube with clay required you go try a few times in order to make it almost perfect.

**3.** Why was it important to measure the sides of the cube?

.................................................................................................................

.................................................................................................................

.................................................................................................................

.................................................................................................................

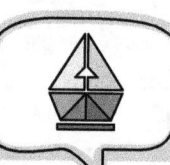
*Yesterday, you explained how some prototypes allow you to improve a final idea or design. Today you will create a prototype of a sneaker out of household materials.*

### Materials:

1. A sneaker or tennis shoe
2. Paper, markers, & colored pencils
3. Cardboard, tape, rulers, clay, aluminum foil, Legos, or any material you could make a model with

### Procedure & Questions:

1. Look at the sneakers or tennis shoes you have. Below list things you like about them as well as thing you want to improve:

| Things I Like: | Things I Want To Improve: |
| --- | --- |
| | |
| | |
| | |
| | |
| | |
| | |

**2.** In the space below, draw a picture of a sneaker that shows at least one change in the design that you wanted to improve. For example, if you want to improve the sneaker by making them easier to put on, you might draw sneakers with velcro instead of shoelaces.

**3.** Now try making a 3-D model of your sneaker design using things like cardboard, legos, aluminum foil or any other craft materials you have in your home. Or use recyclable materials!

**4.** Once you have your model built, take some time to look it over. This is a <u>prototype</u> of your ideal sneaker design. What do you like about it? What would you improve?

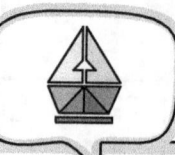
*Yesterday, you designed a prototype for an improved sneaker design. Today you will elaborate on what you noticed about this process.*

**Directions:** Read and answer each question below.

**1.** Why did you write down what you wanted to improve before drawing your sneaker design?

**2.** Why did you draw your design before making a 3-D model?

**3.** Was your model something you could wear?

**4.** If you gave your 3-D model of the sneaker to a real sneaker company and asked them to turn your sneaker from a prototype into a real shoe, what might they need to do?

**5.** Do you think sometimes you need to make more than one prototype or model before you have a final design or solution?

# Answer Sheets

To see the answer key to the entire workbook, you can easily download the answer key from our website!

*Due to the high request from parents and teachers, we have removed the answer key from the workbook so you do not need to rip out the answer key while students work on the workbook.

 To watch free video explanations go to: **argoprep.com/science5** OR scan the QR Code:

**Place your mouse over the workbook you have, and you will see the "Download Answers" button.**

**For detailed video instructions on how to access the "Answer Sheets," please scan this QR code.**

6th Grade Science: Daily Practice Workbook | 20 Weeks of Fun

3rd Grade Science: Daily Practice Workbook | 20 Weeks of Fun...

4th Grade Science: Daily Practice Workbook | 20 Weeks of Fun...

7th Grade Science: Daily Practice Workbook | 20 Weeks of Fun...

5th Grade Science: Daily Practice Workbook | 20 Weeks of Fun...

8th Grade Science: Daily Practice Workbook | 20 Weeks of Fun...

Kindergarten Science: Daily Practice Workbook | 20 Weeks of Fun...

1st Grade Science: Daily Practice Workbook | 20 Weeks of Fun...

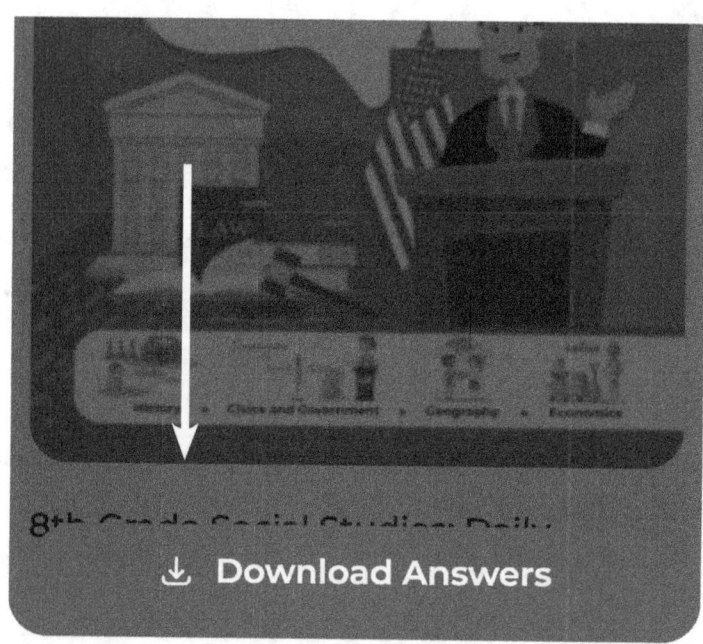

8th Grade Social Studies: Daily

⬇ Download Answers

4th Grade Social Studies: Practice Workbook

www.ingramcontent.com/pod-product-compliance
Lightning Source LLC
Chambersburg PA
CBHW081329120626

46546CB00011B/3267